W9-ASE-567

What People Are Saying about Brian Wills and *10 Hours to Live*...

Are you facing your own "10-hour" situation—an incurable sickness or a circumstance that looks completely hopeless? Get ready: your life is about to change as you read this book!

—*Pastor Andy Smith*
Victory Bible Church, Fredericksburg, Virginia

A great tool for people who need healing.

—*Pastor Kim Carroll*
Cornerstone Church of Lexington, Lexington, Kentucky

10 Hours to Live is an awe-inspiring book of faith in a God who still heals today!

—*Pastor Everett Holloway*
Royal Oak Church, Royal Oak, Michigan

This is a book on healing, but the process can be applied to any area of our lives.

—*Pastor Jimmy McClain*
Shield of Faith Church, Phenix City, Alabama

Brian's testimony is an inspiration to anyone desiring to see and know God as the Miracle Worker. God's goodness is revealed in a great way in this tremendous true story.

—*Charlene Ferguson*
Cofounder, Living Word Church, Richmond, Virginia
Chaplain, Hospice of the Sandias, Clovis, New Mexico

After reading Brian Wills's personal story, coupled with the principles of faith, I have been energized to walk with God at a higher level.

—*Pastor Daniel L. Smith Sr.*
Ahoskie Christian Center, Ahoskie, North Carolina

I would recommend this book to anyone who is searching for the answers to how to get started and how to maintain a successful, rewarding life of faith.

—*Pastor John Pogue*
Freedom in Christ Church, Chambersburg, Pennsylvania

Brian's love for the Lord and people is evident through the book.

—*Pastor Hank Parker*
Grace Alive Outreach Church, Midlothian, Virginia

An excellent book to give to those in need of healing or who want to minister healing to the sick.

—*Pastor Jerry Spurrell*
World Outreach Church, Tulsa, Oklahoma

Brian Wills shares his miraculous "Victory over Death." He does this through his inspiring and uplifting testimony to the powerful sovereignty and healing touch of the living God. What a witness for standing on God's Word. This book will bring healing to many and glory to the living God.

—*The Reverend Canon Kenneth D. Richards*
Anglican Diocese of San Joaquin, California

When I read *10 Hours to Live*, I sensed the anointing. I believe people will be healed as they read this book.

—*Pastor Matt Nalette*
Word Fellowship, Glastonbury, Connecticut

This book will put hope into people's hearts and inspire them to build and exercise their faith to receive healing from God.

—*Pastor Sam Smucker*
The Worship Center, Lancaster, Pennsylvania

Just as Jesus said during His own ministry, "Your faith has made you well," you can see how Brian walked this out in his own life and also learn how your faith can make you well.

—*Pastor Ray Eppard*
Victory Worship Center & World Outreach,
Staunton, Virginia

All I wanted to do after reading this book was to stand and shout, "I shall not die, but live, and declare the works of the LORD." I am the director of the Healing Rooms in our church and someone whom God has healed of cancer, and there will definitely be more than one copy in our library.

—*Pastor Jeffrey G. Evans*
Director, Healing Rooms of Delaware County
Middletown Baptist Church, Media, Pennsylvania

I found Brian's faith so strong that it ministered to me! His testimony and the faith adventure he went through during this time in his life is something everyone should read. As Brian's pastor, I want to recommend his ministry as a speaker for church services, seminars, healing schools, and conferences. His faith and testimony are excellent, and his ability to teach, preach, and minister to others is even greater.

—*Pastor Jim Langlois, D.Min.*
The Master's House, Ashland, Virginia

We believe this book is destined to become a healing classic and a textbook for anyone seeking the healing power of God. God is faithful to every generation, and Brian's miracle is a miracle for all of us to be reminded that God is the same, yesterday, today, and forever.

—*Pastors Randy and Cherie Gilbert*
Faith Landmarks Ministries, Richmond, Virginia

I have seen God work through Brian in a mighty way to bring healing to the sick and suffering. If you are in need of healing or in the healing ministry, this book is a must-read.

—*Pastor Earl Darling*
Yorktown Vineyard, Yorktown Heights, New York

10 Hours to Live is power-packed, inspirational, and instructional. I highly recommend it!

—*Pastor Ray Sensenig*
Grace Fellowship Church, Reading, Pennsylvania

Six years ago, our associate pastor was diagnosed with non-Hodgkin's lymphoma, and we stood on the principles presented in this book. He was cancer-free within a few months.

—*Pastor Mike Legg*
King of Kings Worship Center, Purcellville, Virginia

You are about to read one of the most amazing accounts of the power of God working in one man's life that you will ever encounter.

—*Jack Hicks*
Founder/Director, CURE Ministries, Inc.,
Hagerstown, Maryland

10
HOURS
to
LIVE

10 HOURS to LIVE

A TRUE STORY OF HEALING AND SUPERNATURAL LIVING

Brian WILLS

WHITAKER
HOUSE

Unless otherwise indicated, all Scripture quotations are taken from the *New King James Version*, © 1979, 1980, 1982, 1984 by Thomas Nelson, Inc. Used by permission. All rights reserved. Scripture quotations marked (KJV) are taken from the King James Version of the Holy Bible. Scripture quotations marked (NIV) are from the *Holy Bible, New International Version*®, NIV®, © 1973, 1978, 1984 by the International Bible Society. Used by permission of Zondervan. All rights reserved. Scripture quotations marked (NASB) are taken from the updated *New American Standard Bible*®, NASB®, © 1960, 1962, 1963, 1968, 1971, 1972, 1973, 1975, 1977 by The Lockman Foundation. Used by permission. (www.Lockman.org). Scripture quotations marked (MESSAGE) are taken from *The Message: The Bible in Contemporary Language* by Eugene H. Peterson, © 1993, 1994, 1995, 1996, 2000, 2001, 2002. Used by permission of NavPress Publishing Group. All rights reserved. Scripture quotations marked (NLT) are from the *Holy Bible, New Living Translation*, © 1996. Used by permission of Tyndale House Publishers, Inc., Wheaton, Illinois 60189. All rights reserved. Scripture quotations marked (AMP) are taken from the *Amplified*® *Bible*, © 1954, 1958, 1962, 1964, 1965, 1987 by The Lockman Foundation. Used by permission. (www.Lockman.org). Scripture quotations marked (HCSB) are taken from the *Holman Christian Standard Bible*®, © 1999, 2000, 2002, 2003 by Holman Bible Publishers. Used by permission.

All possible efforts were made by the author to secure permission and to insure proper credit was given for the photos within this book.

Some definitions of Hebrew and Greek words are taken from *Strong's Exhaustive Concordance* or the *New American Standard Exhaustive Concordance of the Bible* (NASC). The Lockman Foundation. Used by permission. The definition of *steadfast* is taken from *Merriam-Webster's 11th Collegiate Dictionary.*

10 HOURS TO LIVE:
A True Story of Healing and Supernatural Living

ISBN: 978-1-60374-243-6
Printed in the United States of America

Brian Wills
Healing for the Nations
info@healing4nations.com
www.healing4nations.com
www.10hourstolive.com

Whitaker House
1030 Hunt Valley Circle
New Kensington, PA 15068
www.whitakerhouse.com

Library of Congress Cataloging-in-Publication Data

Wills, Brian, 1964–
10 hours to live / Brian Wills.
p. cm.
Summary: "Brian Wills relates the true account of his miraculous healing from stage 4 Burkitt's lymphoma—an incurable disease—through faith in God and His Word, and provides biblical guidelines for healing"—Provided by publisher.
ISBN 978-1-60374-243-6 (trade pbk. : alk. paper) 1. Spiritual healing—Christianity. 2. Wills, Brian, 1964– 3. Burkitt's lymphoma—Religious aspects—Christianity. I. Title. II. Title: Ten hours to live.
BT732.5.W499 2010
234'.131—dc22

2010022782

1 2 3 4 5 6 7 8 9 10 11 12 17 16 15 14 13 12 11 10

Dedication

I want to dedicate this book to my parents, Willie and Myrtle Wills. Since childhood, they have instilled in me a strong faith in God and a belief in a miracle-working God.

Thank you, Mom and Dad.

To God be all the glory.

Acknowledgments

When I was battling Burkitt's lymphoma, God sent many people to assist, pray, encourage, and stand with me and my family.

I want to thank Dick and Mary Koester, complete strangers at the time, for opening up their home to my parents and giving them a place to stay. For months, their home became a safe refuge and haven from the storm.

Jim and Tootie Owens and Bob and Betty Anne Howell loaned us their vehicles; the Howells also gave us "Godly Instructions for Healing"; Mandy Gibson provided computer printouts of all the healing Scriptures; and Richard Vaughan and Lennie and Elizabeth Weddle were God's messengers at the appropriate times—they became to us what Aaron and Hur were to Moses. (See Exodus 17:10–13.)

There were many who prayed and stood with us: Pastors Randy and Cherie Gilbert, Lynne and Danny Jordan, Pastors Hank and Patsy Parker, Pastors Jim and Charlene Ferguson, Bob Minor, Ernie Thomas, Sharon Jenicek, Barbara Fraley, the McGrath family, and my friends Tricia, Phil, and Suzy.

I am grateful for the care that I received from many of the doctors, nurses, and housekeeping workers at the National Institute of Health (NIH), and I want to thank my primary doctors, Dr. Zambrana, Dr. Sartor, and Dr. Rosenberg.

I want to thank Pastor Drew Lynch for starting me on this project—he initially contacted doctors, collected the facts, and organized the timeline of the miracle so that it could be presented completely and in sequence.

Finally, I want to thank Melanie Hemry for her help in the writing and editing of the manuscript, following the Holy Spirit from start to finish.

Contents

Foreword

The single most compelling thing about Brian Wills's story is that Brian is here to tell it. He should not have survived. He was the first survivor—and remains the only survivor—of anyone ever diagnosed with stage 4 Burkitt's lymphoma in its deadliest version. Also, not one other patient from Brian's control group at the National Institute of Health in Bethesda, Maryland, who submitted to the experimental Protocol MB-204 in 1987 survived the treatment. Brian was the sole survivor. He was also the only one ever known to have had a "spontaneous remission" even before the protocol was started.

This book is all about surviving. And not just surviving, but overcoming. Admittedly, no one remains alive in this world forever. But too many people are needlessly checking out prematurely, leaving their loved ones heartbroken and their work unfinished.

Brian's story reveals the secret to living a supernatural life that goes from strength to strength in the full allotment of purpose-filled days that God has ordained for each of His sons and daughters. His remarkable experiences demonstrate for the reader how to *take hold of the life that is truly life* (1 Timothy 6:19 NIV), which can carry one triumphantly past the grave into the ages to come.

This story will intrigue cynics and saints alike, but Brian makes no apologies for his faith in God, which is at the center of his indisputable experiences. His kind of living faith is rare, though the seeds that can sprout as a result of it lie waiting to germinate within each one of us. How tragic that so few are able to access that faith when it is needed most. Brian and I hope that retelling this story will do something to change that. Our hope is that you may be able to appropriate healing and experience the goodness of God in the land of the living.

—*Drew Lynch*
Founding Pastor, Eastgate Church of the Nations
New Rochelle, New York

Part I
Victory over Death

CHAPTER ONE

Two-Minute Warning

My hand was moist on the racquet as I slammed an ace across the net and watched my opponent scramble, almost tripping as he missed the ball. At twenty-two, I had almost sixteen years of experience on the tennis court. My serve proved they were years well spent. So did the record I held when I graduated from Drury University: 121 wins—more than any other player in the school's history at that time. Now, as the assistant coach at the University of Richmond, I was training hard for my upcoming trip to Europe, where I would play on the professional satellite circuit.

Perspiration matted my shirt to my back as I sprinted to hit a backhand across the net. In mid-stride, I caught my breath as something like liquid fire snaked across my abdomen. Sweat dotted my upper lip, not from exertion, but from the mind-numbing pain that seared me, licking my insides to a slow burn. I faltered—my steps unsteady, and my hand trembling on the racquet. Gritting my teeth, I decided to take a break and sat in the locker room with my head in my hands. *What's happening to me?*

> *The mind-numbing pain seared me, licking my insides to a slow burn.*

My doctor had said the occasional bouts of pain were the result of overtraining, so I'd cut back on my training schedule. I made sure I got plenty of rest and ate well. But it didn't help. When I least expected it, the fire still roared to life and caught my breath away. Since the pain was in my lower abdomen, close to my bladder, I'd gone to see a urologist.

"It must be in your head," he'd said, dismissing me.

He was wrong. He had to be. There was nothing psychological about the pain that drove me off the court that day. Thankfully, when the pain left my body, it disappeared from my mind. Weeks passed in a blur of activity as I prepared for my flight to Europe. This would be the fulfillment of a lifetime of dreaming and training. I refused to let it be marred by the sudden flames of fire.

Sidelined

My flight was scheduled to depart on Super Bowl Sunday, the last Sunday in January 1987. That week, snow fell in piles so deep that the world looked like it had been iced with a thick layer of whipped topping. I waded out into the snow and let my shovel slice through the drifts that covered the driveway. Bundled against the freezing wind, I worked up a sweat, and, by the time I'd finished clearing away the snow, my back ached, strained by the repetitive work. I fell into an exhausted sleep Friday night but woke around midnight with chills, fever, and pain. Saturday morning, I went to see my family doctor.

"Your blood count is alarming," he said, frowning. "I'm going to admit you to the hospital for further tests."

"But my flight leaves tomorrow!"

It appeared that I would not be on it. My family rallied around me at the hospital. "Nothing's changed except the date you leave," they assured me. "We'll reschedule your flight."

After being admitted to Chippenham Hospital in Richmond, Virginia, I curled up in a fetal position on the bed in my private room and clenched my jaw against the unrelenting back pain. Outside, snow and ice covered the parking lot. Inside, I shook with chills, despite the warmth of the room. My stomach felt full and distended.

Over the next nine days, I suffered through a sigmoidoscopy, a CT scan, a needle biopsy, and multiple blood tests. I was stunned when the tests revealed that my right kidney had stopped working. No wonder my back was hurting! The pain hadn't come from shoveling snow or my training schedule.

"You may have a kidney stone," the doctor said, hazarding a guess.

Each day, family and friends showed up at the hospital to encourage me. At night, when they all went home, and the hustle and bustle of the hospital dimmed with the lights, I lay in bed and pondered my situation. I was a twenty-two-year-old athlete in excellent physical condition. It couldn't be anything serious.

Could it?

The Sentence

On February 6, the ninth day of my hospitalization, my parents, brother, sister, aunt, and uncle were in my room laughing and telling stories when my doctor arrived.

"I have some really bad news," he said, sorrow dimming his kind eyes. "Brian has a mass in his abdomen the size of a golf ball, which has been diagnosed as Burkitt's lymphoma, a rare,

"Brian has Burkitt's lymphoma, a rare, fatal disease. It progresses very quickly."

fatal disease usually found in African children. It progresses very quickly, and there are only three hospitals in the world that treat it. I'm trying to get you into the closest one: the National Institute of Health, NIH, in Bethesda, Maryland."

We must have looked as baffled as we felt.

"Do you have any questions?" the doctor probed.

We couldn't think of a thing to say except that we wanted to go home for the weekend and pray.

"That's fine," the doctor said, "but I must warn you—this is a very fast-growing tumor. It's been known to kill children in a day."

Taking a Stand

The doctor's words hung over the room like a death sentence long after he'd gone. The once-smiling faces of my family members looked stricken. I reeled inside, trying to regain my bearings. How *could* I have a serious illness? I was young and healthy. My whole life stretched before me like a promise.

Some of my family already understood what I had yet to grasp: the tumor was malignant, and I was fighting for my life. I'd been hit hard by a foe called Burkitt's lymphoma.

Our family's quick response to go home for the weekend to pray came as no surprise. We'd always been a close Christian family. Just as my father and grandfather had passed their love of sports down to me, my parents had passed down to us kids a spiritual heritage. They had lived their faith in front of us; they weren't ashamed to let it show. I'd grown up attending the local church and traipsing along with them when they made hospital and nursing home visits. My parents also ministered to young people, and it wasn't unusual for groups of up to forty of them to gather at our house, worshipping God until the wee hours of the morning.

The gospel I'd witnessed since I was a child was not a weak one. I had attended healing services, and I'd seen blind eyes opened. I'd witnessed deaf ears hear again. I'd seen polio victims completely healed. I'd been instantly healed of many childhood injuries, and my parents had dug into spiritual healing a few years before when my mother had been diagnosed with allergies. Later, my father received a diagnosis of cancer. Through it all, we learned that God's Word, written in the Bible, was alive and powerful. We'd also learned the power of our own words. By believing God and confessing His Word over their situations, both of my parents had been healed.

> *The gospel I'd witnessed since I was a child was not a weak one. I'd seen blind eyes opened. I'd witnessed deaf ears hear again.*

I didn't know what Burkitt's lymphoma was, but healing had always come easy for me. I left the hospital ready to receive a miracle.

At home that weekend, as I tried to sleep, I realized that what my doctor had said was true: I was running out of time. Lying on my side, I could see the cancerous mass—now much larger than a golf ball—move as I turned.

Open Doors

While I was trying to receive my healing, my doctor was doing everything possible to get me into the National Institute of Health in Bethesda, Maryland. He was told that there was a six-month wait.

A few months earlier, my doctor had attended a medical conference. During the conference, a physician sitting beside him had introduced himself and given my doctor his card. "I'm at the National Institute of Health," he'd said. "If you run across someone with a very fast-growing cancer, like Burkitt's lymphoma, give me a call. That's my specialty."

On Monday, my doctor called this man, and every door to the NIH swung open for us.

On Tuesday, my parents drove me to Maryland for a consultation. The National Institute of Health was an impressive complex of distinguished-looking buildings housing the newest technology, as well as personnel doing cutting-edge research. By the time we arrived, the pain was so severe I couldn't walk; my family carried me inside.

Ushered into a small room, I was examined by Dr. Young, one of the world's leading authorities on Burkitt's lymphoma. Afterward, he shook his head. "I don't think there's anything I can do for you," he said. "You're too far gone."

Too far gone?

Beaten at the Game of Life

The tumor that had been the size of a golf ball on Friday now measured almost ten inches in diameter. The cancer had spread to my lungs, liver, and most of the organs of my body. "Today is Tuesday, and your son won't be alive by Friday," the doctor explained to my parents. "I'll admit him to the hospital and keep him as comfortable as possible." He stepped out of the room to make the necessary arrangements.

I felt like I'd been shoved over a precipice and was hurtling toward destruction at breakneck speed. I didn't know how to stop my fall. My life had spiraled out of control.

It was my mother's words that slowed my descent and set me on solid ground again. "No, God's Word says that by Jesus' stripes, Brian is healed. *'Let God be true, and every man a liar.'*" (See Isaiah 53:5 KJV; Romans 3:4 NIV.)

"Let God be true, and every man a liar," we all agreed.

"We're going to make our stand right now and believe God, no matter what the doctors say," she announced.

In my mind's eye, I saw a football game in progress. One team was whipping the other when I heard a two-minute warning. I realized that, so far, my team was being beaten by Burkitt's lymphoma, and there was a two-minute warning in my life. The game wasn't over yet, but I knew that without a miracle, I would never make it out of the hospital alive.

CHAPTER TWO

The Death Ward

An orderly wheeled me up to my room on the thirteenth floor of the NIH—the ward reserved for incurable patients. The only way anyone left was by way of the morgue. The long corridor buzzed with activity. The first thing I noticed was that the patients suffered from uncommon diseases; many of their faces were enlarged, their bodies disfigured. An air of hopelessness and despair hung over the ward like a shroud. The cancer patients in particular had a hollow look.

I am surrounded by death, I realized.

Once I was settled into my room, I discovered that everyone, including my roommate, a young man in his thirties, talked incessantly about his diagnosis, his disease, his prognosis, and what his doctor had said.

The Lord told me to steer clear of such talk: *Son, if you allow yourself to think the way they're thinking and speak the way they're speaking, you will get the same results they're getting.* The hairs on the back of my neck stood up, and I shivered at the warning. My words had to line up with what God said in the Bible.

In Deuteronomy 30:19, God said,

> *I call heaven and earth as witnesses today against you, that I have set before you life and death, blessing and cursing; therefore choose life, that both you and your descendants may live.*

I had a choice to make. I could believe God for my healing and go after it like a starved animal in search of a meal, or I could get depressed and believe what the doctors were telling me. I could think and meditate on God's Word, which brings life, or I could dwell on my diagnosis and prognosis, which would lead to death.

> **I had a choice to make. I could believe God for my healing, or I could get depressed and believe what the doctors were telling me.**

I couldn't afford to waste a single moment, a single thought, or a single word. I clung to Proverbs 4:20–22:

My son, give attention to my words; incline your ear to my sayings. Do not let them depart from your eyes; keep them in the midst of your heart; for they are life to those who find them, and health to all their flesh.

Single-Minded

The way I read those verses, my healing depended on keeping the Word of God before my eyes every waking moment of the day. Some might consider such an interpretation extreme. But, when I was lying on my deathbed, the Bible looked pretty black-and-white. If ever there was time to get serious about obeying God, this was it. My family helped out by papering the walls of my hospital room with computer printouts of Bible verses that offered healing promises. (An expanded version of those healing Scriptures can be found in Part III of this book.) We each made a firm decision to immerse ourselves in the Bible and make sure all our words agreed with God's. We refused to speak negative words of doubt, unbelief, or fear.

I understood that to say one thing and try to believe another was being double-minded, and the Bible says that a double-minded man will receive nothing from God. (See James 1:6–8.) I needed a miracle, and I wouldn't get it by being double-minded. Curled up in a fetal position, writhing in pain, it was a hard line to hold. Pain meds helped me get enough relief to stand my ground.

A Catholic priest walked the halls offering patients their last rites. He paused at the doorway of my room and looked inside. *You've got the wrong room*, I thought.

"I think you've come to the wrong room," I said, teeth gritted against the pain. "You must be looking for someone down the corridor."

The Countdown

The Burkitt's lymphoma accelerated at warp speed, invading most of my organs and muscles. At regular intervals, the medical staff measured the tumor in my abdomen. Each time, it had taken another menacing step forward toward my demise. The cancer was an unforgiving and relentless foe.

Later that day, my doctor examined me and reviewed my test results.

"Your right kidney hasn't worked for weeks, and your left kidney won't be able to function much longer," he explained. "It's so overworked that it could rupture anytime. Your cancer is growing by the hour, and I don't know if you'll make it until morning." The doctor turned to my parents and said, "I give him ten hours or less to live."

Ten hours or less to live.

Time stood still. The earth stopped spinning on its axis and skidded to a stop in its celestial tracks. Too stunned to speak, I looked out my hospital room window and thought, *I'll never step outside and feel the wind on my face again. I'll never play the European circuit. I'll never hit another tennis ball. What will my dog think when I don't come home?*

My parents followed the doctor outside to talk to him, and I prayed a "foxhole" prayer. "Lord, I know that You're my Healer; I've seen You heal people all my life. I don't understand what's going on. I need wisdom. I need Your help. My life is Yours; save it, and I'll serve You forever. I'll go wherever You want me to go; I'll do whatever You want me to do."

> *The still, small voice of God came like a whisper.* **Son, I am your Healer.**

The still, small voice of God came like a whisper of wind blowing through my heart. *Son, I am your Healer, and I will manifest healing to you as you take the steps I tell you to take. You will walk through the fire and not be burned.*

For the first time, I realized that there was something for *me* to do. I had a part to play in the process. "Lord," I prayed, "You said there were steps. Tell me the first one."

One word welled up within me.

Forgive.

The First Step

In my heart, I saw a person's face from my past and knew that I must be harboring unforgiveness toward him. It had been so long since I'd seen the person, I'd lost track of him.

"Lord, I don't even know how to reach him."

A phone number marched across the recesses of my mind. A few hours later, I reached for the phone on my bedside table and dialed the number. The person answered. I asked for forgiveness and healed the breach in our relationship, never mentioning that I was on my deathbed.

That night, the one the doctors had predicted would be my last on earth, seemed to hang in eternity. The wall clock ticked away the minutes and hours while I waged war against fear. "Have you made your funeral arrangements yet?" my admitting nurse had asked earlier. The words swirled around me like a dervish, trying to torment me.

Still awake, I heard the soft soles of the night nurse padding across my room. I glanced at the clock. *I'm still alive,* I thought, knowing she'd come to see if that was the case. Turning on the light, she spoke to me before checking my vital signs, my intravenous medication, and my output.

"Oh, my gosh!" she gasped. "Your kidney has started working!"

She hurried out to phone my attending physician, Dr. Oliver Sartor.

When the sun peeked over the horizon, I drew a deep breath and realized that I'd just received two miracles. My kidney had started functioning again. And I was still alive.

> *"Your kidney has started working!" the nurse gasped.*

None of the doctors could understand why I had lived through the night. I could only imagine their response if I'd said, "It's because I forgave someone." The only explanation they gave was that I was in excellent physical condition, and it was taking longer for me to die than most. Certain that I would pass away at any moment, the medical staff watched and waited. I spent the next two days asking God to reveal any remaining unforgiveness, sin, bitterness, or resentment in my life.

As the Lord brought different situations to my mind, I remembered the Lord's Prayer, especially the words, "Forgive us our sins, as we forgive those who sin against us." (See Luke 11:4.) I knew that was only one of many Scriptures that linked the forgiveness of our own sins to our willingness to forgive others. I repented of every offense that the Lord brought to my mind, getting my heart right with God.

Dealing with Death

When I'd done all the repenting I knew to do, I asked God for the second step in my healing process. He answered me by bringing a Scripture passage to my mind. I opened my Bible to Malachi:

> *"Will a man rob God? Yet you have robbed Me! But you say, 'In what way have we robbed You?' In tithes and offerings. You are cursed with a curse, for you have robbed Me, even this whole nation. Bring all the tithes into the storehouse, that there may be food in My house, and try Me now in this,"* says the LORD *of hosts, "if I will not open for you the windows of heaven and pour out for you such blessing that there will not be room enough to receive it. And I will **rebuke the devourer** for your sakes, so that he will not destroy the fruit of your ground, nor shall the vine fail to bear fruit for you in the field."* (Malachi 3:8–11, emphasis added)

The devourer is the devil, or Satan, and the Bible says that he is the one who steals, kills, and destroys. (See John 10:10.) My life was being devoured like scrub grass in a forest fire. If anyone ever needed God to rebuke the devourer for him, I was that person. As I meditated on that passage of Scripture, my heart stuttered with sudden understanding.

I'd been out of college and on my own for only about six months, and I hadn't been tithing. I wrote down a figure and gave it to my parents, asking them to withdraw the amount from my checking account and give it to the church.

Having done that, I believed that God would do what He promised. He would deal with the devourer who was trying to kill me.

Fighting Fear

Fear haunted the halls of the thirteenth floor. It stalked us during the dark hours after midnight when most of us couldn't sleep. It bombarded me with thoughts that exploded like missiles of terror in my mind. *You're going to die. Prayer won't work this time.*

For days, I fought fear more than I fought cancer. It was like a noose trying to strangle me, torment me, and lie to me. Fear tried to play my funeral over and over in my mind. I knew I couldn't lie in bed each night and allow fear to run rampant with torment. I had to defeat fear if I was ever going to defeat cancer, so I began to take every fearful thought captive and replace it with faith.

> *I began to take every fearful thought captive and replace it with faith.*

"Fear," I said, "I resist you in the name of Jesus. God has not given me a spirit of fear, but of love and power and a sound mind. Satan, I rebuke you! You can't take my life! I will live and not die! I will declare the works of the Lord!" (See 2 Timothy 1:7; Psalm 118:17.)

The spirit of fear didn't just give up and leave me alone; it attacked me hundreds of times, and, each time, I took authority over it and confessed the Word of God over my situation. Following each battle, I would finally experience peace and drift off to sleep.

During all this, my tumor had grown to the size of a basketball, and my circumstances appeared grim. *Don't believe the circumstances,* I warned myself over and over. *Believe God.*

I doubled my efforts to speak Bible verses over myself. "No weapon formed against me will prosper," I read aloud. (See Isaiah 54:17.) "The enemy that comes against me one way will flee before me in seven directions." (See Deuteronomy 28:7.) I tried to focus more on the Bible than on the fact that my abdomen protruded as if I were nine months pregnant.

Using the authority that Jesus gave the believer, I commanded cancer to leave my body.

The hospital sent me an unending parade of psychologists, social workers, nurses, and doctors determined to prepare me for imminent death. I grew to dread their questions, careful to answer them only with Scripture verses.

"Have you made your funeral arrangements?"

"No," I said, forcing myself to smile, "I believe I will live and not die, because by Jesus' stripes I was healed."

"How are you coping?"

"I believe that no weapon formed against me will prosper," I replied.

"You need to accept the fact that you're dying."

They didn't understand that I would *never* accept that fact because it was not what God said in the Bible. They didn't understand that healing was part of the salvation Jesus bought on Calvary. They didn't understand that I couldn't just give in to sickness, accept it as God's plan for me, and pray, "Thy will be done." They didn't understand that the Bible declares God's will for me is healing, and that to receive that healing, I had to believe God's Word—no matter what.

They wrote in my chart that I was in denial.

They wrote the facts about my physical condition.

But God's Word is truth, and truth can change the facts. (See Psalm 119:160; John 17:17.)

I staked my life on it.

Friday came and went, and I lived to see it.

Game Over

For the next several days, I made steady improvement. My kidneys continued to function. My distended abdomen decreased in size. The pain subsided. The greatest sign of improvement—I was still alive.

My doctors were stumped. They couldn't figure out why I was alive or why I was improving, and several medical students were assigned to my case to determine the reason behind the sudden and apparent change in my condition. "I can't explain it," my doctor said. "I think we'll try a pre-dose of chemotherapy. It will give us an idea of how your body might respond to the chemotherapy protocol."

> *"Brian, we don't understand what's happening with you."*

On February 20, after the pre-dose of chemotherapy, my doctor ordered another CT scan.

That evening, he came back to my room clearly perplexed. "Brian, we don't understand what's happening with you. While you were getting your CT scan, the radiologist called and said that they'd checked you from head to toe three different times, and you were NED."

What is NED? Near Extreme Death? I had no idea what he was talking about.

Heart hammering in my ears, I asked, "What's NED?"

"It means No Evidence of Disease. There's no longer a tumor in your abdomen. No cancer in your liver, lungs, or muscles. No cancer in your kidneys or brain. There's no trace of Burkitt's lymphoma in your body! And we have no explanation."

> *"There's no trace of Burkitt's lymphoma in your body!"*

I took a deep breath and felt the earth slowly spin on its axis again. I looked from the doctor's stunned face to the world outside my window. I would leave this place. I would live and not die. With only two minutes remaining on the clock, God had kicked the devil all the way down the field and out of the stadium.

He had defused the time bomb in my body.

I'd received a miracle.

CHAPTER THREE

The Protocol

Joy washed over me in waves and spilled out through the emotions I'd been holding under firm control. Between gales of laughter, I spoke back to my mother the words she'd declared over me when I'd been diagnosed.

"'Let God be true, and every man a liar'!" (Romans 3:4 NIV).

"'Let God be true, and every man a liar'!" she agreed, laughing, as we both praised the Lord. I felt like I'd been standing before a firing squad whose guns had failed. I felt like I'd been a condemned man sitting in the electric chair when the power had gone out. The reprieve was indescribable, my joy complete.

The same God who had parted the Red Sea for the Israelites had performed a miracle for me. The same God who had raised Jesus from the dead had infused my body with resurrection life. The God of the universe had touched me.

> *The same God who had raised Jesus from the dead had infused my body with resurrection life.*

I thought of Jesus turning water into wine at a wedding feast. The same power that had exploded inside those water molecules, changing them into wine, had detonated in my body, bringing healing and health.

The Bible says that God watches over His Word to perform it. (See Jeremiah 1:12 NASB.) That verse came alive for me in a fresh way. I imagined that the first thing on

God's to-do list each day was *Watch over My Word to perform it.*

I, Brian Wills, by the power of almighty God, was about to leave floor thirteen of the NIH, the Death Ward, as no other Burkitt's lymphoma patient ever had: alive and well.

Friendly Fire

I wanted to dance. I wanted to sing. I wanted to pack my bags and get out of this place, never looking back. We were still celebrating and preparing to leave when my doctor came back with a group of other physicians.

"We have a huge decision to make now," he said.

I stopped packing my bags, perplexed. "What decision?" I asked.

"Whether or not to proceed with chemotherapy," he answered.

"I'm *healed*—why would I need chemotherapy? There's no evidence of disease in my body. You said so yourself."

"Yes, that's true," he admitted with reluctance. "But Burkitt's lymphoma is so deadly that if there is even a single cell left somewhere in your body, it could come back. That's why we've decided that you need to stay and be treated with our new protocol."

My mother and I exchanged stunned glances. *No. There's no need for any protocol*, we agreed without uttering a word.

The doctors were intent on convincing us of the wisdom of the idea.

We weren't buying it. It just didn't make sense to get chemotherapy *after* I'd been healed.

They pulled out all the stops in an effort to convince us to stay and receive their treatment.

We finally agreed.

We would question that decision many times in the months ahead.

Support Groups

Once we realized that I would be at the NIH for a long time, family friends pitched in again to help. Jim and Tootie Owens and Bob and Betty Anne Howell loaned us their cars. Dick and Mary Koester, a couple my parents met in Maryland, welcomed them into their home, where they would stay for months.

There were six other young men, all roughly the same age, at the NIH with the diagnosis of Burkitt's lymphoma. Stages of cancer are numbered from 1 to 4, with 4 being the worst. I'd been labeled 4B on admission—the worst and final stage of cancer. The others in the group were all at stages 1 or 2. They were already receiving the experimental chemotherapy protocol MB-204, which I was about to start.

I soon bonded with the other men in the group. One of the favorite pastimes of the patients on our ward was to delve into the NIH's extensive medical library. I realized that for me, however, it would be a trap. I didn't want to focus on the negative medical reports. I wanted to keep my attention on what God had to say about my health and healing. So I refused to spend my time there.

With my lengthy hospital stay looming ahead, my entire family had to make changes. My mother opted to put her whole life on hold and stay with me. My dad returned to work, but his employer allowed him to put in four-day workweeks so he could drive the two- to two-and-a-half-hour trip from our home in Richmond, Virginia, and spend the weekends with me in Baltimore. My brother moved back home to help my dad during the week. My sister spent her lunch breaks fasting and praying for me. Burkitt's lymphoma had sidelined my whole family, while our friends and neighbors' lives moved on as usual. In addition, the fear associated with cancer caused many friends to turn away from us, as if they thought they might be contaminated if they got too close.

Even so, I was fortunate, and I knew it. Some of the patients on my ward were alone, their families thousands of miles away. They had no support group, no one to lean on except the staff. My heart ached for them. I lay in my bed amazed that there were people suffering with life-threatening diseases in hospitals every day.

A Strategy

It was a frigid day in February, and the blustery wind was whipping against the barren trees outside my hospital room when my mother bustled in, bundled in coat and gloves, a wide smile across her face.

"The Lord gave me the first step in our chemotherapy strategy," she told me. "He said that we're to pray over every dose of medication you receive and ask that it do no harm to your body."

> **The Lord showed us that I should immerse myself in the Scriptures.**

"Sounds good to me," I agreed.

The second strategy the Lord showed us was that I should immerse myself in the Scriptures. In addition to avoiding the medical library, we were impressed to avoid all television and to limit visitors.

In preparation for the battle ahead, my mother wrote all my healing Scriptures on three-by-five cards. She also brought a tape recorder so that I could listen to recordings of the Bible or praise music around the clock.

When I started the chemotherapy protocol, my mother and I slipped into our own routine. My job was to make sure my doses of God's Word exceeded my doses of MB-204. More Scripture than chemo. That was my goal each day.

"He *'healed all who were sick,'*" I confessed, "*'that it might be fulfilled which was spoken by Isaiah the prophet, saying: "He Himself took our infirmities and bore our sicknesses."'* Matthew eight, sixteen and seventeen."

I continued, "*'Who Himself bore our sins in His own body on the tree, that we, having died to sins, might live for righteousness; by whose stripes you were healed.'* First Peter two, twenty-four."

"*'I am the LORD who heals you.'* Exodus fifteen, twenty-six."

I confessed many such Scriptures several times a day. I praised the Lord and listened to the Bible on tape. For the first two weeks of the chemotherapy, I had very few side effects. After praying and confessing Scripture, I spent my free time getting to know other patients on the ward.

A Hiding Place

One by one, I saw other patients on the floor waste away and die. The buzz on the ward was who was dying and who had died. People died often, and death was so pervasive that my room became my sanctuary.

There, surrounded by praise music and the Scriptures, I felt like I was in the *"secret place of the Most High"* described in Psalm 91:1. The atmosphere of death tried to suck the life out of me, but I resisted it and praised my way into the presence of God.

One evening, a doctor stepped into my room and paused. "There's something different about this room," he said. People may not have known what to call it, but they felt the manifest presence of God that inhabited my praise. (See Psalm 22:3 KJV.)

> *The atmosphere of death tried to suck the life out of me, but I resisted it and praised my way into the presence of God.*

My mother prayed over every dose of chemotherapy and every drug that went into my body from early morning until she left the hospital to sleep. During the night, I prayed over them.

Although on the outside I seemed okay, inside, I chafed against the confinement of the hospital. I felt like someone had pressed the Pause button on my life; everything was on hold. No playing the European circuit, no training schedule, no hanging out with my friends, no going to church or playing ball with my dog. I was wrapped in a world filled with death and dying, IVs and potent drugs, hospital food and mourning people.

But I was alive. I needed to keep an attitude of gratitude. Life, even life at the NIH, was better than an early grave.

As days passed with no negative side effects from the drugs, I heard more and more horror stories from the nurses and other patients. I soon understood why the Bible says that we are to be careful about what we hear. Such stories of pain and grueling death could spark fear in the bravest hearts. At nighttime, that fear became like a monster that crept out of closets and from under beds. It was a terrorist that persisted in its brand of torment. When panic welled up inside, I turned on the lights to drive the monsters off. While the clock ticked away the hours, I read the Scriptures on my wall until I was filled with peace. Then, finally, I drifted off to sleep.

As a precaution, the doctor ordered two days of radiation to my brain. Radiation was a degrading and difficult experience for me. I hated the smell and the red dots on my head. Each time I went for radiation, I took Charles Capps's mini-book, *God's Creative Power*, and confessed the Scriptures over and over.

Fighting Back

Two weeks into chemotherapy, my body reacted violently. I heaved as spasm after spasm of nausea racked my stomach. I couldn't keep anything down and lost strength at an alarming rate. I shivered under the covers, feeling miserable.

Between spasms of nausea, I confessed, *"'So you shall serve the* LORD *your God, and He will bless your bread and your water. And I will take sickness away from the midst of you. No one shall suffer miscarriage or be barren in your land; I will fulfill the number of your days.'* Exodus twenty-three, verses twenty-five and twenty-six."

> **Between spasms of nausea, I confessed, "'And I will take sickness away from the midst of you.'"**

I stumbled to the bathroom and heaved into the toilet. When I got back in bed, my mother wiped my face with a damp cloth as I continued. *"'No evil shall befall you, nor shall any plague come near your dwelling....With long life I will satisfy him, and show him My salvation.'* Psalm ninety-one, verses ten and sixteen."

I didn't make it to the bathroom this time.

Limp with exhaustion, I crawled back into bed, saying, "*'Bless the* Lord, *O my soul, and forget not all His benefits: who forgives all your iniquities, who heals all your diseases.'* Psalm one hundred and three, verses two and three."

Clearly, I would not sail through chemotherapy on a cloud of glory. The battle had been joined.

And I was already almost too sick to fight.

CHAPTER FOUR

Death by a Different Name

Heat radiated from my skin like steam from a sidewalk on a scorching summer day, but, inside, I quivered like a rabbit caught in a snowstorm without shelter. My teeth chattered as a night nurse wrapped me in ice blankets.

"Your temperature is one hundred and five," she said, tucking the freezing blankets around me. "That's high enough to fry an egg, and it could fry your brain."

"What's wrong with me?" I asked, stammering with chills.

"The chemotherapy has wiped out your immune system," she explained. "That's why your body gets infections so easily. What you've got now is one of the worst. It's called *candida*. It's like having a systemic yeast infection. Most people die within hours when they have it as bad as you do."

She told story after story of patients with candida she'd treated who had died. In an attempt to block out her words, I turned my head to one side and tried to focus my eyes on the Scriptures posted on my wall. As her voice droned on, I read the words, too weak to make a sound.

> *Then Jesus went about all the cities and villages, teaching…, preaching…, and healing every sickness and every disease among the people.* (Matthew 9:35)

"Fighting" Faith

The long night wore on, and in the morning, my mother arrived with hope shining in her eyes and faith wrapped around her words. My fever raging, I shook too hard to hold the three-by-five cards. I was too weak to read them. "I can't do it anymore," I said, begging to be left alone.

"Brian, you have to do this," my mother insisted. "I'll read the words, and you repeat them after me."

"'Beloved, I pray that you may prosper in all things and be in health, just as your soul prospers.' Third John, verse two."

Voice raspy, teeth chattering, I repeated the words.

"'Is anyone among you sick? Let him call for the elders of the church, and let them pray over him, anointing him with oil in the name of the Lord. And the prayer of faith will save the sick, and the Lord will raise him up. And if he has committed sins, he will be forgiven.' James five, verses fourteen and fifteen."

Stammering, I repeated each word, letting it sink into my soul.

"'Therefore I say to you, whatever things you ask when you pray, believe that you receive them, and you will have them. And whenever you stand praying, if you have anything against anyone, forgive him, that your Father in heaven may also forgive you your trespasses. But if you do not forgive, neither will your Father in heaven forgive your trespasses.' Mark eleven, verses twenty-four through twenty-six."

Saying those words and remembering how forgiveness had caused my kidney to start functioning strengthened my faith to fight.

Each Friday, I experienced the changing of the guards. That's when my mother would leave her post and go home for a few days, and my father would arrive for a long weekend. Each of my parents brought his or her own brand of strength, and one of my dad's strengths was his positive attitude. A man unashamed of love, he didn't hesitate to tell me how he felt.

"Brian," he said as he watched me suffer, "I'd give anything in the world if I could take this for you. But I'm eternally grateful that Jesus already did. He suffered for you on Calvary, and He made you whole. Don't give up."

A Subtle Attack

Weeks passed, but my body couldn't kick the infection that still raged. Nurses stood on either side of me, sponging my skin in an attempt to lower my temperature.

"I really don't know why you're still alive," my doctor said.

Through dry, cracked lips, I whispered, "I will live and not die."

He glared at the Scriptures on my wall. "That's just it, Brian. You're *not* going to live through this; nobody could. I've already explained that to you. You're in denial about death, and that's what I'm writing on your chart."

> *Through dry, cracked lips, I whispered, "I will live and not die."*

He stormed out of the room, his lab coat swishing behind him.

In the wee hours of the following morning, the night nurse told me that they had to move me to another room. Too sick to object, I let them pack my belongings and roll me to another room on the same ward. They didn't take the Scriptures posted on the wall. When my mother arrived the next morning, she looked for them in my old room and asked the nursing staff what had happened to them.

They'd apparently been discarded by the staff.

The NIH is the mecca of the medical community. There is no more respected hospital and research center in the nation.

Yet, they had little use for the Bible, my Scripture verses, or faith in God. That fact became apparent again and again.

It seemed to be a battle between science and faith. The psychologists were always questioning our faith, every day.

The battle was mostly with the atheists and scientifically trained doctors. Each night, when my mother left the hospital, she asked the nurses to keep the audiotapes of the Bible she had brought to me playing throughout the night so I could hear the Word around the clock. The nurses did comply at times by helping to turn over the audiotapes in the middle of the night. I had audiotapes of healing Scriptures, praise and worship music, and teaching tapes on healing.

Yet, on three different occasions, I was moved to a different room in the early hours of the morning. Each time, the computer printouts of my Bible verses were either lost or discarded by the staff. Each time this happened, my family responded by printing more.

Once, the doctor took my parents out into the hall to talk to them, and then he came back to talk to me alone. "I don't get it!" he said, seething with frustration. "You all say the same thing! None of you is coping with reality! You all have serious psychological problems!"

Facing the Giant

A psychologist was sent to my room twice a day. It seemed to me that his sole mission was to undermine my faith. Packed in ice and still fighting a raging fever, I steeled myself when he entered my room.

"May I bring a video camera and ask you some questions on film?" he asked.

"Why do you want to do that?"

"When you die, I want to show it to people who come here praying for a miracle. It's for everyone who believes in God, because there's *not* a God. He doesn't exist. This video will be proof to them that after all of your prayers for a miracle, they won't help, and you'll die."

I couldn't believe what I was hearing. *Why on earth would anyone try to convince a patient to quit and throw in the towel when one of the strongest deterrents to death is our will to live?* It didn't make any sense. Staring at the man, I thought back to my old tennis coach, Dan Cashel. "The moment I see you quitting, I'd rather pull you off the court than let you stay in and lose," he'd threatened. Battling cancer was a lot like a tennis match. For someone to make it, he had to have a fighting spirit. Even if the medical odds were against me, after years of competitions, I knew one thing for sure: It's not over until it's over.

"The Bible says that by Jesus' stripes I was healed," I said, wanting nothing more than to shiver in silence.

Enraged, the doctor grabbed my hospital gown and shook his fist in my face. "If there *was* a God, what makes you think that He'd heal *you* when everyone else is dying?"

With that, he stormed out of the room.

Still shivering, I knew what I had to do if I wanted to walk out of the place alive. Offense was a trap of Satan, and I had to walk in love and ignore his insults, because faith works by love. (See Galatians 5:6 KJV.) No matter how many times they told me I was crazy, removed my Scriptures from the wall, or wrote in

> *I knew what I had to do if I wanted to walk out of the place alive. I had to forgive and keep forgiving.*

my chart that I had psychological problems, I had to forgive and keep forgiving.

Kicking It Up

In the third week of the candida infection, my temperature still soared, and I lay packed in ice. Tears ran from the corners of my eyes and dripped onto my pillow. My throat raspy, I whispered, "I'm so sick, Mom, I just can't do it anymore. I can't even say the Scriptures."

She wrapped her arms around me, and we both wept.

When she returned the next morning, I explained the strategy God had given me during the night. "I'm getting enough of God's Word in me to stay alive in spite of the infection," I said. "But I'm not getting enough of the Word in me to throw it off. The Bible says that God's Word is medicine to our flesh, but, right now, the infection and I are equally matched; neither of us has the strength to overcome the other. In order to survive, I have to find a way to beat the infection, and that means I have to increase the time I spend in the Word—no matter how awful I feel."

With that realization, I kicked myself into high gear, spending two-and-a-half to three hours a day confessing a single verse—such as 1 Peter 2:24—one thousand times. I also started reading an additional two chapters of the Bible each day—one in the morning and another each evening.

A Clean Sweep

Still, my hair fell out by the handfuls, and I lost so much weight that I appeared skeletal. Sweat from high fevers kept my bedding soggy. Embarrassed by the hair loss and the mess in my room, I watched with profound gratitude as a lady on the hospital housekeeping staff fought to keep my room neat and my bed clean.

"I can't tell you how much we appreciate all that you do," my mother said to her one morning. "Please accept this as a token of our appreciation," she added, handing the housekeeper some money.

"Oh no, I couldn't!" she insisted.

"Is there *anything* that we could do to bless you?" my mother asked.

The lady looked at the floor for a long moment before answering. "Well, there is one thing that would bless me very much."

"What is it?" my mother asked, eyes dancing.

The woman looked at the computer printout of healing Scriptures on my walls. "These," she said with reverence. "Could I have a copy of these verses?"

A Golden Gift

We almost wept for joy, not just because of what the woman was doing to help me, but because at last we'd found one person at the NIH who valued those Scriptures as a gift of great worth. If we ever doubted her sincerity, those doubts fled the day we presented her with her own copy of the Bible verses. She acted as though we'd given her gold. And, indeed, we had. As Psalm 19:9–10 says, *"The judgments of the LORD are true and righteous altogether. More to be desired are they than gold, yea, than much fine gold."*

Although the NIH had given me the best medical care available at that time, we had been persecuted by some there for our faith. What a blessing it was now to have a friend walking the halls of the hospital! How encouraging to know that, in addition to her thoughtful care in cleaning my room, she esteemed the Word of God as much as we did.

I would need all the help I could get.

CHAPTER FIVE

Living in the Secret Place

The snow melted and the redbuds blossomed as winter gave way to spring. The morning sun splashed across my room with a hint of warmth that, on a normal day, would have left me stretching my muscles and yawning with sleepy delight. Instead, I watched in shock as my body flopped around on my hospital bed like a fish thrown into the bottom of a boat. I willed myself to stop jerking, trying with all my strength, but the convulsions were out of my control. A nurse stepped into the room, turned, and ran to get help. Within minutes, six doctors surrounded my bed, watching me with bemused expressions on their faces.

"What do you think is causing that?" one doctor asked as I continued to convulse.

"I don't know," the second doctor said, turning to a third. "What do you think?"

They still pondered the situation, and my body still trembled and jerked, when my mother stepped into the room. "Doctors, what's going on?" she asked.

"We don't know," one of them admitted.

"Do you mind if I step in for a minute?"

"Not at all."

My body still flopping, I watched my mother put down her things and crawl onto my bed. Strange as it may seem, while my body was out of control, my mind was clear and calm. What my mother did next reminded me of the story in the Bible about Elijah praying for a boy who had died. He crawled on top of the child and prayed for him. I was stunned when my mother lay on top of me and declared, "In the name of Jesus Christ, I command this body to stop convulsing right now! I speak peace over my son's body, in Jesus' name!"

As soon as she finished praying, my body stopped shaking.

"Okay, Mom, you can get down now," I said.

The doctors still circled my bed with shocked expressions on their faces. "What did you do?" one of them asked.

She told me later that the moment she stepped into the room, the Lord showed her that I was having a reaction to one of the drugs, and she proved to be right. The Lord knew the interactions of those drugs better than the doctors did.

Laughter, the Best Medicine

A few weeks later, I was alone in my room when I reached for a cup and lost my balance. I fell, landing with my head on the floor and my feet on the bed. I struggled to pull myself up, but I'd lost so much muscle mass that I didn't have the strength. Exhausted, weak, and weary, I felt as helpless as a baby. I wanted to weep, but I knew that the Bible says that we are surrounded by *"a great cloud of witnesses"* (Hebrews 12:1 NIV). Among them, I was sure, was the devil and his crowd. I didn't want to give them the pleasure of seeing me cry, but, lying on the floor too weak to get back in bed, what else could I do?

A Scripture welled up in my heart. *"A merry heart does good, like*

> *I wanted to weep, but a Scripture welled up in my heart. "A merry heart does good, like medicine, but a broken spirit dries the bones" (Proverbs 17:22).*

medicine, but a broken spirit dries the bones" (Proverbs 17:22). I knew that I needed a good dose of medicine that could come only through a merry heart. I have to admit, I didn't *feel* merry. I felt awful. I felt like I had one foot in the grave, and the rest of me was on a slow, downward slide. But I also knew that this wasn't just a physical battle; it was a spiritual one. And although I knew a lot about God's character and very little about the character of the devil, there was one thing I knew with certainty: the devil *hates* to be laughed at.

Lying there with my head on the hospital room floor, I did one of the hardest things I'd ever done in my life. I made myself laugh. "Ha-ha," I croaked. "Ha-ha-ha-ha!" *The devil's not going to have the last laugh*, I thought. *I am.* "Ha-ha-ha-ha-ha-ha-ha!"

In spite of my situation, I got tickled. What began as a forced laugh eventually became a real one. A while later, a shocked nurse stepped into the room and found me lying on the floor, laughing with deep belly laughs. She helped me to bed, but I couldn't quit laughing.

Wow, I thought between gasps, *I can't remember the last time I laughed this hard or felt this good.* Laughing at the devil was just the medicine I needed; the more I laughed, the stronger I felt.

Washing of the Water of the Word

One day during my prayer time, the Lord showed me two pitchers of water. One pitcher was small with dirty water in it. The other was a large, crystal pitcher filled with clear water. "Lord," I asked, "what does the small pitcher of dirty water represent?"

It represents your body being attacked by cancer. The large, crystal pitcher represents My Word. If you will pour the larger pitcher into the small one, you will be healed by the washing of the water of the Word.

That mental picture of the pitchers helped me to stay focused on saturating myself with and immersing myself in the Word. I understood that the law of displacement would cleanse my body of any deadly thing. I found that it took a lot of Scripture to overcome the constant barrage of doubt and unbelief that permeates such an environment.

> **Psalm 91 contains some of the most powerful promises of protection found in the Bible.**

As I meditated on the Word of God, one portion that took on special meaning for me was Psalm 91. This psalm contains some of the most powerful promises of protection found in the Bible. It tells us that we can dwell in physical safety anytime, anywhere, if we'll live in what the Bible calls the *"secret place of the Most High."* It says,

> *He who dwells in the secret place of the Most High shall abide under the shadow of the Almighty. I will say of the LORD, "He is my refuge and my fortress; my God, in Him I will trust." Surely He shall deliver you from the snare of the fowler and from the perilous pestilence. He shall cover you with His feathers, and under His wings you shall take refuge; His truth shall be your shield and buckler. You shall not be afraid of the terror by night, nor of the arrow that flies by day, nor of the pestilence that walks in darkness, nor of the destruction that lays waste at noonday. A thousand may fall at your side, and ten thousand at your right hand; but it shall not come near you. Only with your eyes shall you look, and see the reward of the wicked. Because you have made the LORD,*

who is my refuge, even the Most High, your dwelling place, no evil shall befall you, nor shall any plague come near your dwelling; for He shall give His angels charge over you, to keep you in all your ways. In your hands they shall bear you up, lest you dash your foot against a stone. You shall tread upon the lion and the cobra, the young lion and the serpent you shall trample underfoot. Because he has set his love upon Me, therefore I will deliver him; I will set him on high, because he has known My name. He shall call upon Me, and I will answer him; I will be with him in trouble; I will deliver him and honor him. With long life I will satisfy him, and show him My salvation. (Psalm 91)

As I meditated on the truths in those verses, they became my reality. Even while my hair fell out and my body wasted away, I found that I could hide away in God's divine comfort and shelter. And there, despite the onslaught of symptoms, my life was protected. As all the other patients with Burkitt's lymphoma succumbed to the illness, I claimed the Psalm 91 promise that *"a thousand may fall at your side, and ten thousand at your right hand; but it shall not come near you"* (verse 7).

I longed for those around me to make the same claim. After all, the promise wasn't just for me. It was for every patient at the NIH. It would work for anyone who would believe and trust in it. Through faith in God's Word, they could find, just as I had, the entrance into that secret place where no pestilence—or cancer—could kill.

In the midnight hour, when fear and death stalked the ward, I whispered, "I will say of the Lord that He is my refuge and fortress, my God, in whom I will trust."

You're going to die, the devil taunted.

> *The battle was waged as much in my mind and heart as in my body. Staying in the Word of God and in an attitude of prayer was my best offense.*

"I will not be afraid of the terror by night, nor of the arrow that flies by day," I declared.

The battle was waged as much in my mind and heart as in my body, so there was no part of me—spirit, soul, or body—that could take a break from the unrelenting siege that had been set against me. I found that staying in the Word of God and staying in an attitude of prayer were my only defense and my best offense.

Weapons of Warfare

One New Testament story that encouraged me in a special way was the account of the persecution encountered by Paul and Silas, apostles of the early church. They were thrown into a physical prison no less perilous than the prison of sickness and disease that we at the NIH experienced. Acts 16 tells us what happened:

> *Then the multitude rose up together against them; and the magistrates tore off their clothes and commanded them to be beaten with rods. And when they had laid many stripes on them, they threw them into prison, commanding the jailer to keep them securely. Having received such a charge, he put them into the inner prison and fastened their feet in the stocks. But at midnight Paul and Silas were praying and singing hymns to God, and the prisoners were listening to them. Suddenly there was a great earthquake, so that the foundations of the prison were shaken; and immediately all the doors were opened and everyone's chains were loosed.*
>
> (Acts 16:22–26)

Like the residents of the thirteenth floor of the NIH, Paul and Silas suffered their most fearful time at midnight. They were in total darkness, with their hands and feet bound, but instead of caving into fear, they...*sang praises to God!* The Bible says they sang so loud that all the other prisoners heard them. In response to their praise, God sent an earthquake and opened the prison doors.

Praise Is the Key to Your Prison

Inspired by that story, I learned to praise my way through many sleepless nights, certain that God would rescue me just as He'd rescued Paul and Silas. Through my midnight hours, I tried to keep an attitude of gratitude toward God. I can't say that it was easy to praise Him when I couldn't keep any food down, but I can say that it was crucial. Psalm 149:5–6 says, *"Let the saints rejoice in this honor and sing for joy on their beds. May the praise of God be in their mouths"* (NIV). Praise is the key that opens every prison door.

I also discovered that the secret to maintaining a spirit of praise in such a situation lay in keeping my eyes on the God-given vision of victory and health I had in my heart. In a crisis situation, most people focus on the outside; they focus on symptoms and circumstances. I learned that if I was going to survive, I had to ignore the outward manifestations, as gruesome as they were, and keep my attention fixed on God's Word. I knew that I couldn't afford to let myself think thoughts of sickness. I had to see my healing first in the Bible, and then I had to see myself victorious—alive, well, and healed. When I was

> *I had to see my healing first in the Bible, and then I had to see myself victorious— alive, well, and healed.*

too sick to raise my head off the pillow, I visualized myself playing tennis again. I also kept a picture beside my bed showing me well and vibrant with good health.

While I believed that the picture would one day be a physical reality, I was so emaciated that walking across my hospital room felt like running a marathon. But as spring ripened into summer, I gained enough strength that I was given a pass to leave the hospital.

It seemed like a lifetime since I'd felt a breeze on my face and the sun warm my cheeks. For my first outing, my mother packed a picnic and pushed me outside in a wheelchair. While I had refused to weep from the defeat of falling out of bed, now I couldn't stop the tears of joy. The sun anointed me like a warm cloak as I drank in the sights and sounds of *life*. I thrilled at every bird singing in the trees; I marveled at the flowers, which looked like works of art brushed by God's hand just for our enjoyment; I soaked in the noises of traffic, distant voices of children laughing—all the sights and sounds that I had taken for granted most of my life.

I was too weak to walk across the vivid, green grass, but that didn't stop my joy. Months before, I'd been given ten hours to live. I might have been emaciated and weak, but I was *alive*. God in His faithfulness had granted me a miracle.

Life instead of death; hope instead of despair.

After all those months, the doctors were still expecting me to die. They were waiting for it with the same perplexed looks on their faces as they'd had when I was convulsing. They couldn't understand why I was alive because the answer was not explained in any of their textbooks. The answer to my survival could be found in only one Book—the Bible, which they did not believe or esteem.

Death Stalks

Although I rejoiced over every hour and every new day, one by one, all my friends on the ward died. It wasn't easy to put all my faith in the Word of God and ignore the death that surrounded me, but I understood that it was my only hope. As long as I had breath in my body, I would keep rejoicing in the Lord and fighting to live.

As time wore on, I was granted more passes to leave the hospital for a day and even a weekend, and each of those excursions felt like a reprieve from death row. The first time I was allowed to go home for the weekend, it felt like a dream come true. I sat in the car and watched the familiar landmarks as we drove. Inside the house, I paused, dizzy with the sights, sounds, and smells that meant home. I breathed in the faint scent of furniture polish and felt the comfort of my favorite chair.

I was home, a place the doctors had said I would never see again. Each visit was a healing balm for my soul and a comfort to my weary body. Back at the NIH, my mother and I found a church to attend. After months of near isolation, I felt enveloped in corporate praise and worship. Never had the Word of God preached from a pulpit been so precious to me; never had I been so in awe of God.

Independence Day

On July 4, 1987, six months after I should have died, I watched fireworks through the fourteenth-floor windows of the NIH and celebrated my own victory. The doctors could say what they wished, but they couldn't deny the reality that, against all odds, I was still very much alive. To me, the splash of brilliant colors against the night sky symbolized my praise, thanksgiving, and worship to God. My heart felt like it could explode in praise to Him with its own cacophony of sound and flash of light.

That summer, I began walking through malls to build my stamina. Walking was a painful experience due to the drug-induced neuropathy in my hands and feet. I started with no more than a work/rest program, walking a few feet and resting, but in my mind, I saw myself strong and healthy, dashing across the tennis court to slam a ball over the net.

> *In my mind, I saw myself strong and healthy, dashing across the tennis court.*

When I'd begun the chemotherapy protocol, I'd been the only patient diagnosed in stage 4B—the very last and worst stage of the fast-growing cancer. My continued survival had created a conundrum for the doctors as each of the other men in stages one and two died. As a result, I was chosen as the patient to represent the NIH in its new brochure. Photographers were dispatched to take my picture, and I was labeled the miracle poster patient for the NIH.

Discharged from the NIH

During the last three rounds of chemotherapy, I suffered no infection and was allowed to spend most of my time at home, driving to the NIH for treatments. I finished the last dose of chemotherapy protocol in August, and I was still standing.

"Burkitt's lymphoma grows so fast," my doctor explained after my last treatment, "that if it's going to come back, it will be within the next three months."

I knew I was healed but wanted to cement my victory, so

in September I traveled to Tulsa, Oklahoma, to the campus of Rhema Bible Training Center and attended a two-week healing school. There, the instructors taught daily from the Scriptures about healing, and at the end of those two weeks, they prayed for those of us in the class. The following month, I was the best man in my brother's wedding. Standing beside him in my tuxedo, it felt as though someone had punched the Play button. Once again, my family and I could live our lives. We could move forward without the daily threat of my impending doom.

On November 3, I arrived back at the NIH for my three-month checkup. "Things look promising," the medical staff told me. "We're gratified with your progress and cautiously optimistic."

Okay, I wanted to say, *you gave me ten hours to live, and it's been ten months! You said if the cancer returned, it would happen within three months of stopping the chemotherapy protocol. It's been three months, and I'm still here!*

Two Miracles

In February 1988, one year from when I'd been admitted, I returned to the NIH for my six-month checkup. After examining me from head to toe, Dr. Rosenberg said, "Brian, there's something that you need to know. We gave you seven drugs that were experimental and had never been researched or tested. Now that we've had time to test them both in the lab and in experimental use, we've learned some things. We now know that the drugs which made up the protocol we gave you don't even treat Burkitt's lymphoma. But that's not all. The drugs themselves are so lethal that we've discontinued their use. The drugs killed everyone we gave them to...except you.

"So let me explain: you were healed of Burkitt's lymphoma with no known medical explanation—the disease just disappeared from your body. In addition, you survived months of being injected with lethal drugs. We have no medical explanation for your standing here today."

> **"We have no medical explanation for your standing here today," the doctor said.**

I was the only survivor of MB-204.

I was the only survivor of Burkitt's lymphoma.

I had no illusions that I deserved to live any more than the others had deserved to die. I knew that the only reason I was still alive was that I had saturated myself in God's Word. I had believed His Word above my diagnosis and all the wisdom of this world, including that of the National Institute of Health.

I walked outside the NIH and listened to the sounds of a dog barking in the distance, car horns honking, and a flag rustling as it was whipped by the wind. I stood, drinking in the sights and sounds, so amazed at the power of God. I imagined how the Israelites must have felt when they walked on dry land through walls of water. I imagined the awe they experienced when those same waters covered the army that pursued them. They saw the walls of Jericho fall at a shout and the blast of a ram's horn. They saw the miracle of God's provision in the desert—manna on the ground for them to eat and water pouring forth out of a rock for them to drink.

Cars zipped past as I crossed the street, and crowds of people hurried along the sidewalk. I wondered how many of them knew that there is a God who still performs miracles. I wondered if they knew that God watches over them, sings over them, and loves them with an everlasting love.

I wondered if they realized that God is still in the miracle business, and that His power is available to them today.

I stopped and turned my face to the sun, taking a deep breath. I knew that for the rest of my days, I would tell whoever would stop long enough to listen.

Courtesy of Drury University

Brian (pictured in bottom left corner) with the Drury University tennis team

Courtesy of Drury University

On the courts at Drury University

Brian as the "miracle poster patient" for the NIH

Heading to Europe after being miraculously healed to spend the summer playing
tennis against some of the world's best players at competitions in Germany,
Holland, France, and Switzerland

With friends on the European pro circuit

Playing in the European pro circuit

Brian and his wife, Beth

Brian and Beth with their children,
Emily, Madeline, Preston, and Jessica

Brian and Madeline

Ministering healing around the world…

CHAPTER SIX

Living a Supernatural Life

I raced across the tennis court, jumped, and slammed the ball over the net. *Score!* I lifted my racquet high and leaped with sheer joy as my muscles stretched, invigorated by the game. Wiping perspiration off my face, I jogged over to shake hands with my opponent. Following the competition, I stood outside my hotel and gazed at the Swiss Alps, which stood with timeless majesty against a topaz sky. The air was sweet with the scent of orchids, geraniums, and a rainbow of blossoms I could not name. I felt a lot like those plants lifting their heads toward heaven and coming to life, blooming after a long hiatus.

I'm here, I thought for the millionth time, resisting the urge to pinch myself. Just a few months earlier, I'd had my one-year checkup at the National Institute of Health. By May, after working hard to regain my strength, I'd begun playing professional tennis again. Now, I was spending the summer playing against some of the world's best tennis players at competitions in Germany, Holland, France, and Switzerland.

For so long, my life had hung in the balance on the thirteenth floor of the NIH. My world had revolved around hospitals, drugs, doctors, and death. Those long months spent fighting for my life had changed me in subtle ways. The things most people take for granted—a beetle crawling up the rugged, charcoal terrain of tree bark, a butterfly fluttering on the breeze, the sound of laughter, the scent that wafts from a nearby bakery, and a thousand other delicious sensations—made every moment a treasure.

The miracle that began in me when God healed me from Burkitt's lymphoma had morphed into my playing professional tennis on the European circuit. I knew, and everyone who knew me knew, that from a natural standpoint, I shouldn't have been anywhere except six feet under. My playing professional tennis again was nothing short of a miracle.

> *From a natural standpoint, I shouldn't have been anywhere except six feet under. My playing tennis again was nothing short of a miracle.*

I was living my dream in Technicolor, grateful for every ball I rallied across the net, humbled by the aches and pains not caused by sickness but by muscles that had been resurrected to live again. If that weren't enough, I'd even been given the opportunity to play in the qualifying tournament for Wimbledon. Once, that would have been the culmination of all my dreams, but over the past couple of years, my priorities and passions had changed. While I still loved tennis—the fierce concentration, the intense physical exertion, the adrenaline rush, the speed and the competition—there was an ache in me that none of those things could fill.

All over the world, in quiet hamlets of Germany, beneath the Swiss Alps, in Amsterdam, in Africa, in Guatemala, in the United States—and, heaven knows, in the National Institute of Health—people were dying before their time because they didn't know there is a God who still performs miracles. Of the millions who knew God, only a scattered few understood how to receive a miracle from Him.

Tennis was fun, but people were dying—and I knew the antidote. God had replaced the burning flames of cancer that had once raged in my body with another kind of fire: a blazing desire to stand between the dying and the grave and help them connect with the healing power of God. So, instead of playing further competitive tennis, I changed the direction of my life. In 1990, I moved to Tulsa, Oklahoma, to attend Rhema Bible Training Center. Two years later, I graduated and stepped into a world of hopeless, hurting people, feeling inadequate to help but knowing that *"with God all things are possible"* (Matthew 19:26; Mark 10:27).

We serve a God of miracles; the same God who raised Jesus from the dead is still performing miracles every day. But there is a miracle that is greater than blind eyes seeing, deaf ears hearing, paralyzed limbs moving, or tumors disappearing. It's the miracle that occurs when you ask Jesus into your heart, and your spirit is raised from the dead and given immortality. It's the miracle that not only guarantees you eternal life in heaven with Jesus but also opens the door to a supernatural life right here on earth.

> *God had replaced the burning flames of cancer with a blazing desire to stand between the dying and the grave and help them connect with the healing power of God.*

If you would like to receive this miracle, simply pray this prayer:

> Father God, I repent to You for all my sins. I thank You that Jesus died on the cross in my place, and I accept Your great gift of forgiveness. I ask Jesus

to live in my heart, direct my steps, and teach me to walk in Your ways. In the name of Jesus, I pray. Amen.

It's been more than twenty years since God healed me of Burkitt's lymphoma and the lethal drugs used to treat it. When I was discharged from the National Institute of Health, my doctor warned me that the treatment had rendered me sterile. Today, my wife, Beth, and I have four children. I travel the world telling anyone who will listen that God still performs miracles. I am so grateful to Him for healing me and for allowing me to help other people receive their miracles.

For me, witnessing blind eyes see, deaf ears hear, tumors dissolve, and the dying resurrected to new life is far better than winning Wimbledon. It's greater than winning the Grand Slam. Those victories last for a moment; these last for a lifetime.

The greatest miracle of all lasts for eternity.

I know this about God: What He's done for me, He'll do for you. If you're sick, He will heal you. If you're hopeless, He will give you hope. And if you want to live a miraculous life, it is available to you—today.

Part II
Steps to Healing

Introduction

Christianity is based on miracles. The virgin birth, turning water into wine, walking on water, healing the sick, and raising the dead are all miracles that occurred in the life of Jesus Christ, who is God incarnate. Our God is a God of miracles; He is a miracle-working God. If anyone should believe in and experience miracles, it should be those of us who are God's people.

I'm saddened to report that in many churches today, there is still little or no teaching on healing and miracles. Yet, that is the gospel that Jesus preached and delivered to us. (See, for example, Matthew 10:7–8; Luke 4:18; Luke 10:1, 8–9.) Too often, we've settled for a form of godliness while denying its power. (See 2 Timothy 3:5.) However, those days are over. You are about to discover not empty words but the power of God locked in the Scriptures.

People often hear or read about a miraculous story but don't realize what went on behind the scenes in order for a person to possess that miracle. I'm often asked, "What steps did you take to receive your healing?" There are many hurting people today who don't know what to do or where to start to receive their miracles.

Part II of this book is a more in-depth, behind-the-scenes look at what our family did and the steps the Holy Spirit gave us in regard to healing, as well as examples of healing in the lives of others. At the time of my diagnosis, our family had never faced such a difficult test of faith. My father, mother, brother, and sister all rallied together to believe God for a miracle. Our church family and friends also rallied and were a great encouragement to us.

It is my prayer that the following pages will be a practical guide to help you navigate through difficult circumstances and to know what to do in case you or someone you know needs a miracle. I believe that you will discover the God who heals and receive all that has been provided for you through Jesus Christ.

CHAPTER SEVEN

Step One:
<u>Have Faith in God</u>

"[Jesus said,] *'Have faith in God.'*"
—Mark 11:22

Your image of God has a lot to do with whether or not you receive from Him. Since the very beginning, Satan has sought to cast a shadow on God's character. The enemy seeks to distort and pervert God's image in the minds of God's creation. He is a deceiver. (See John 8:44.) He knows that if he can get you to believe a lie about God, then you won't put your trust in Him and approach Him with faith and confidence.

Years ago, I was in Nairobi, Kenya, listening to the street preachers on every corner. A small circle of thirty to forty people would gather around each one to hear him preach, but as I listened to the various messages, I realized that nearly all of them were preaching on judgment and hell.

The image they presented of God was that He was a condemning deity, ready to send them to hell. While there is a heaven to gain and a hell to shun, God never created hell for man. Hell was created for Satan and his fallen angels. I wanted to interrupt the sermons of these street preachers and tell the people the most important thing they needed to know about God: He's *good*!

You are good, and what you do is good; teach me your decrees. (Psalm 119:68 NIV)

> *Oh, taste and see that the* LORD *is good; blessed is the man who trusts in Him!*   (Psalm 34:8)

Love Never Fails

A few years ago, a man with AIDS came to a healing service and received prayer for healing. Weeks later, he was tested and the doctors discovered there was no evidence of the virus in his body. He came back to the church and testified of his healing. When he did, he asked the pastor, "Why did God heal me? Doesn't He know that I have been such a bad person?" The pastor said, "God did not heal you because you have been a bad person, but He healed you because He is a good, good God."

> *"God did not heal you because you have been a bad person, but because He is a good God."*

It is the goodness of God that draws men to repentance. (See Romans 2:4.) How many of us can testify to His goodness!

One way to keep your doctrine straight and your attitudes and actions Christlike—no matter what circumstances you face—is to always remember these truths:

1. God is good.
2. The devil is bad.
3. They never change roles.

Once, I preached in an open-air marketplace in Nairobi and told the people about the goodness of God. A lady came up to me and said, "I'm the local witch doctor, and I've served Satan for eighteen years. Satan has been a hard taskmaster. He has afflicted me with eight diseases and he won't heal me. If what you're saying is true, that God is good, I would rather serve Him. You said Jesus was the Healer. If Jesus will heal me, I will gladly renounce Satan and accept Christ."

When I reached out my hand to pray for her, the power of God hit her, and she was immediately healed. After checking her body, she realized that she'd been healed of not just one but all eight of the diseases that had plagued her. She stepped up to the platform, renounced Satan, and asked everyone in the marketplace to forgive her. Addressing the crowd, she said, "God is a good God. You need to serve Jesus!"

Today, many people are stuck in a spiritual rut because, at some point in their lives, they blamed God for something the devil did to them. They've been hurt and angry at God ever since. And now, they have become bitter.

You must know that sickness comes from Satan and that healing comes from God. It is God's will for us to be healed.

Many are asking, "Who can show us any good?" Let the light of your face shine upon us, O LORD. (Psalm 4:6 NIV)

Many people don't question God's *ability* to heal, but they question His *willingness* to heal. They know God can do anything. Their question is, *Will He do it for me?*

As a parent raising four children, it's important to me that my children know how much I love them and that I want the best for them. My children have no doubt that I'd do anything to help them at any time, especially when they're in need. I'd rather my children understand my willingness to bless them than understand my ability to bless them. I may not always have the resources they need, but they know my nature and character; therefore, they never doubt my willingness to help them.

If that is true of us as parents, how much more is it true of our Father God? He is able, but He is also willing.

If you then, evil as you are, know how to give good and advantageous gifts to your children, how much more will your Father who is in heaven [perfect as He is] give good and advantageous things to those who keep on asking Him!

(Matthew 7:11 AMP)

F. F. Bosworth said, "Faith begins where the will of God is known....Each individual sufferer must be convinced by the Word of God that his or her healing is the will of God."[1]

Personal Revelation

> **We must each have a personal revelation of Christ as our Healer.**

Jesus stated, *"With men it is impossible, but not with God; for with God all things are possible"* (Mark 10:27).

That is an absolute truth. It is not subject to opinion or debate. The truth is that all things are possible with God! However, we don't receive from God based upon His ability—what He *can* do. We receive from God based upon personal revelation of *who He is*. We must each have a personal revelation of Christ as our Healer.

Jesus asked His disciples, *"Who do men say that I, the Son of Man, am?"* (Matthew 16:13). Then he asked them, *"But who do **you** say that I am?"* (verse 15, emphasis added). Peter answered, *"You are the Christ, the Son of the living God"* (verse 16).

---

[1] F. F. Bosworth, *Christ the Healer* (New Kensington, PA: Whitaker House, 2000), 100, 99.

Then, Jesus said,

> *Flesh and blood has not revealed this to you, but My Father who is in heaven. And I also say to you that you are Peter, and on this rock I will build My church, and the gates of Hades shall not prevail against it.* (Matthew 16:17–18)

It's important that you truly understand this. Jesus said that He would build His church upon the personal revelation of who He is. People don't need *information* as much as they need *revelation*.

"Aunt Susie's" Story

I'm often asked questions like, "Why didn't Aunt Susie get healed? She was a wonderful saint who loved the Lord. She was a pillar in the church!"

First, we don't receive from God based on works. If you know anything about the Bible, you must know that salvation can't be earned. It's a free gift that is granted based on our faith that Jesus paid the ultimate price for our sins. *"For by grace you have been saved through faith, and that not of yourselves; it is the gift of God"* (Ephesians 2:8).

We cannot be good enough to earn salvation. So, why do we try to fall back into works where healing is concerned? There are no good works that can earn healing for you or anyone else. Jesus purchased it by the stripes He bore, and that free gift can be accessed only through faith.

Second, "Aunt Susie" may have been a wonderful saint who loved the Lord, but she may have had no knowledge about healing and how to *receive* from God. The Bible says that people perish because they lack knowledge. (See Hosea 4:6.) To be healed, you must receive a personal revelation of Jesus the Healer.

In a ministry service several years ago, twenty people came to the altar to receive prayer for healing. I started to pray for them, but the Lord stopped me, saying, *No, don't pray for them. Tell them to lift up their hands and say, "Jesus, You are my Healer!"*

I gave those instructions, and all twenty people raised their hands and cried out to God, "Jesus, You're my Healer! Jesus, You're my Healer! Jesus, You're my Healer!"

All of a sudden, the presence and power of God fell on that place. God began to touch people while they wept, shook, and fell to the floor. Then, people testified to the miracles they'd received. From the testimonies we heard that day and throughout the next week, I believe all twenty people were healed.

Jesus was blunt about the futility of people trying to obtain anything eternal through works. I like the way His words read in *The Message* Bible: *"No chance at all if you think you can pull it off by yourself. Every chance in the world if you let God do it"* (Mark 10:27).

The Nature of God

God has existed since the very beginning. He has always been who He is, and He has spent thousands of years revealing His character and His nature to human beings. For example...

> *The LORD is merciful and gracious, slow to anger, and abounding in mercy.* (Psalm 103:8)

> *The thief does not come except to steal, and to kill, and to destroy. I have come that they may have life, and that they may have it more abundantly.* (John 10:10)

In spite of God's revelation of His character and nature, many people blame Him for sicknesses, accidents, and calamities, calling them "acts of God." But God is not the author of those things.

Many people who claim to know God don't really know Him at all. Faith in God begins by having faith in *who God is*. However, if you listen to many preachers, you might get the wrong impression about His character and His will.

The church I grew up in taught me that Jesus was the Savior of the world, but it never taught me that Jesus was the Healer. The church was silent and almost discouraging in the area of healing. I was told that miracles were not for today, that they ceased with the last apostle.

Yet, Jesus' ministry consisted of teaching, preaching, and healing the sick. Aren't we to be doing the same works today? Haven't we been given the Great Commission: *"Go into all the world and preach the good news to all creation"* (Mark 16:15 NIV)? Jesus said, *"And these signs will follow those who believe:...They will lay hands on the sick, and they will recover"* (Mark 16:17, 18), and *"Most assuredly, I say to you, he who believes in Me, the works that I do he will do also; and greater works than these he will do, because I go to My Father"* (John 14:12).

> "I am the LORD who heals you" (*Exodus 15:26*).

In the Old Testament, God revealed Himself as Healer. When the Israelites crossed the Red Sea and came to bitter waters at Marah, God said, "I am Jehovah Rapha," which means, *"I am the LORD who heals you."* (See Exodus 15:22–27.) In essence, He wanted them to know that He would be their doctor as they traveled through the wilderness. He turned their bitter waters into sweet waters, and He'll do the same for you.

Maybe you or someone you know have come to bitter waters and received a bad report. If that's the case, God wants to reveal Himself to you as your Healer, but this is how spiritual principles work: *God will become to you who you declare Him to be.* He will turn the bitter waters into sweet waters. He will heal you of whatever sickness or disease you have suffered. *"Nothing is impossible with God"* (Luke 1:37 NIV).

Your Image of God

In the book of Mark, we read,

> *Now a leper came to Him, imploring Him, kneeling down to Him and saying to Him, "If You are willing, You can make me clean." Then Jesus, moved with compassion, stretched out His hand and touched him, and said to him, "I am willing; be cleansed."*
>
> (Mark 1:40–41)

Jesus made His will clear. He said, "I am willing." Yet, today, many people still don't understand God's will.

Everyone has an idea about God's nature; these ideas are formed through things we are taught or come to believe through various experiences and impressions in our lives. It's a monumental mistake to try to ascertain God's character, will, and ways through experience alone rather than by reading the Bible. In fact, painful experiences can cause us to reach wrong conclusions about God that do not agree with Scripture at all. Remember that, since the beginning, Satan has sought to deceive mankind into believing lies about God and His nature. Why does he do that? He knows that as long as you believe a lie about God, you will never experience His true goodness.

Let's look further at what the Bible says about God and His character.

What Is God's Essential Nature?

God Is Love

The Scripture tells us that God Himself is love.

And we have known and believed the love that God has for us. God is love, and he who abides in love abides in God, and God in him. (1 John 4:16)

The most important thing you can say about God's love is that He loves *you.* His love for you is personal and genuine. It is not fickle or flimsy. It is abiding. His love does not wane or fade. It is stable and intense, and it desires the very best for you.

God's nature is love. Every loving parent who has ever had a sick child would do anything in his or her power to get that child feeling better and well again. How much more is this true of our heavenly Father who loves us? God doesn't put sickness on us. He has no sickness. *He came to give us life, and life more abundantly!* (See John 10:10.)

Watch what God does, and then you do it, like children who learn proper behavior from their parents. Mostly what God does is love you. Keep company with him and learn a life of love. Observe how Christ loved us. His love was not cautious but extravagant. He didn't love in order to get something from us but to give everything of himself to us.

(Ephesians 5:1–2 MESSAGE)

God Is Good

A second vital aspect of God's nature is that He is good. Much wrong doctrine in the church stems from the teaching that God uses sickness, tragedy, and devastation to teach and mold His children. It creates much confusion for the believer who is trying to do the will of God because he is never sure whether to resist or to embrace adversity.

Some people say, "Maybe God is putting sickness on me to teach me a lesson." No! That would be like a parent intentionally sticking a child's hand in the fire to teach him or her about fire. That would be child abuse, and God doesn't abuse His children.

God's goodness is seen in the good gifts He gives us. *"Every good gift and every perfect gift is from above, and comes down from the Father of lights, with whom there is no variation or shadow of turning"* (James 1:17). Read a few additional passages of Scripture that attest to God's goodness, and let that truth sink down deep into your heart.

> *Oh, give thanks to the LORD, for He is good! For His mercy endures forever.* (Psalm 136:1)

> *O taste and see that the Lord [our God] is good! Blessed (happy, fortunate, to be envied) is the man who trusts and takes refuge in Him.* (Psalm 34:8 AMP)

> *I'll make a list of God's gracious dealings, all the things God has done that need praising, all the generous bounties of God, his great goodness to the family of Israel—compassion lavished, love extravagant. He said, "Without question these are my people, children who would never betray me." So he*

became their Savior. In all their troubles, he was troubled, too. He didn't send someone else to help them. He did it himself, in person. Out of his own love and pity he redeemed them. He rescued them and carried them along for a long, long time. (Isaiah 63:7–9 MESSAGE)

The truth is that sickness doesn't come from God. Sickness is a work of the devil. (See, for example, Acts 10:38; 1 John 3:8.) God hates sickness. *"[Jesus] went about doing good and healing all who were oppressed by the devil, for God was with Him"* (Acts 10:38).

God Is a Giver

Third, God is a giver. *"God so loved the world that He gave His only begotten Son"* (John 3:16). The greatest act of love is to give. God gave His best. He gave His only Son. The Scripture says that if God was willing to give us His only Son, *"will He not also with Him freely and graciously give us all [other] things?"* (Romans 8:32 AMP). You know that if God was willing to give us Jesus, then He is certainly willing to heal our bodies and to meet all of our needs!

God is not a withholder. *"No good thing will He withhold from those who walk uprightly"* (Psalm 84:11). Remember the patriarch Job? Job's troubles came from Satan (see Job 2:7), though Job struggled over the idea that God was the source of them. When Job saw the light, he repented, and it was God who turned his captivity and gave him twice as much as he had before! (See Job 42:10.)

> **If God was willing to give us Jesus, then He is certainly willing to heal our bodies.**

When I was diagnosed with cancer, one thing I was sure of was that God is good. I also knew that *"He is a rewarder of those who diligently seek Him"* (Hebrews 11:6). I knew that if I sought the Lord with all of my heart, He would reward me by healing my body.

God is love. God is good. God is a giver. He is still giving His blessings to us today.

A Superior and Superabundant Life

God wants us to experience life that is superior in quality and superabundant in quantity. God is not a condemning God. He is not a big Judge in the sky waiting to send a lightning bolt on you every time you miss the mark. In Christ, He has provided forgiveness for your sins and help for your weaknesses. You must have the right image of God in order to receive from Him.

If Jesus said "I am willing" to the leper, He is saying "I am willing" to you.

If you have received a negative report from the doctor, you don't have to accept that report. While sickness in a body may be medical fact, God's Word is the truth. Truth trumps facts. Facts change, but truth always remains. The psalmist said, *"The entirety of Your word is truth"* (Psalm 119:160), and Jesus prayed to the Father for His disciples and all who would believe in Him through their testimony, *"Sanctify them by Your truth. Your word is truth"* (John 17:17). God is the only constant force in the entire universe, so have faith in God!

Whenever you put God in the equation, the equation changes. No sickness, no situation, is too hard for Him. *"With men it is impossible, but not with God; for with God all things are possible"* (Mark 10:27; see also Mark 9:23).

The prophet Jeremiah declared, *"Heal me, O Lord, and I shall be healed; save me, and I shall be saved"* (Jeremiah 17:14).

Step One: Have Faith in God

We can make the same declaration today. Having faith in God means that you have faith in His character. Put your faith in God today, for with Him, all things are possible.

CHAPTER EIGHT

Step Two:
<u>Attend to God's Word</u>

*"My son, attend to my words....For they are life unto those
that find them, and health to all their flesh."*
—Proverbs 4:20, 22 (KJV)

When I was first diagnosed with Burkitt's lymphoma, our family made a decision to believe for a miracle. Time was absolutely critical; the cancer in my body was growing by the hour. We opened the Bible and began to pore over the Scriptures. I never realized at the time how many healing promises the Bible offers. We decided to believe the Bible no matter what the doctor said or how bad the circumstances appeared.

The first thing God says to do is to *attend* to His words. That means you have to *give your full attention* to what God has said. If you're in a battle, and you expect to win, you have to make God's Word your top priority.

The kingdom of God operates on the basis of planting seed. Jesus said,

> *This is what the kingdom of God is like. A man scatters seed on the ground. Night and day, whether he sleeps or gets up, the seed sprouts and grows, though he does not know how. All by itself the soil produces grain—first the stalk, then the head, then the full kernel in the head. As soon as the grain is ripe, he puts the sickle to it, because the harvest has come.*
>
> (Mark 4:26–29 NIV)

If you want a healing harvest, you must plant healing seed. To start your healing, therefore, you must gather all the healing Scriptures in the Bible. Read them, meditate on them, and say them over and over. By doing this, you are planting healing seed in your heart and watering it with your words.

Too often, people wait around thinking that if God wants to heal them, then healing will just "drop" on them. *That's not how spiritual laws work!* God operates on the basis of faith, as we saw in the previous chapter. You might say that faith is the currency of the kingdom of God. You must use your faith in order to receive anything from God. (See Hebrews 11:6.)

"He Sent His Word and Healed Them"

The Bible says, *"He sent His word and healed them, and delivered them from their destructions"* (Psalm 107:20). Your healing will manifest as you combine your faith with God's Word. That's why we kept healing Scriptures in front of us at all times while I was standing in faith for the manifestation of my healing. Proverbs 4:20–21 says, *"My son, attend to my words....Let them not depart from thine eyes; keep them in the midst of thine heart"* (KJV). We had healing Scriptures on index cards at my bedside, on posters, and on the computer printouts on the walls.

> *Your healing will manifest as you combine your faith with God's Word.*

There have been breakthroughs in medical research, as some studies have proven that faith is a determining factor in people's ability to heal. People of faith generally are more positive, heal faster, and recover more quickly than those without faith. While this factor is relatively new to medical research, it is a spiritual law that has been wrapped in the wisdom of the Bible from the beginning.

Years ago, God gave instructions to Joshua on how the Israelites were to possess the Promised Land. He told them,

> *This Book of the Law shall not depart from your mouth, but you shall meditate in it day and night, that you may observe to do according to all that is written in it. For then you will make your way prosperous, and then you will have good success.* (Joshua 1:8)

The Key to Success—Meditating on the Word

The key to success that God revealed to Joshua was meditating on His Word, and it is one of your keys to success, as well. Researchers have discovered the power of meditation. Proper imagery causes the brain to release antibodies and enzymes that fight disease and strengthen the immune system.

God's words are *"life to those who find them, and health to all their flesh"* (Proverbs 4:22). The Hebrew word translated *"health"* also means "medicine." We can therefore make the statement that God's words are medicine. In my case, I realized there was no medicine in the natural that could cure me, but God said His words were medicine and would cure me. God's medicine has no adverse side effects, and no matter how much you take, you can never get too much!

As you gather your healing Scriptures, think about them and say them out loud over and over. Realize that as you do, you're taking God's medicine.

Take God's Medicine

While I was a patient at the NIH, my family and I knew we were in a life-or-death battle. Recall that we didn't allow visitors to come and socialize much. We couldn't afford to become distracted because we had to stay focused and give our full attention to taking God's medicine. There were times when I was too tired or too sick to take it on my own. During those times, others would read verses of Scripture to me. Later, when I was stronger, I would take one verse and recite it over a thousand times in a single day. I was taking God's medicine! That's what you should do, as well.

Over the years, in working with people who were sick, I've witnessed the power of God's Word in action. One example is a woman named Michelle. She was in a coma and on life support, and her kidneys had failed. Michelle desperately needed a kidney transplant, but she was low on the donor list. The doctor explained that she wouldn't survive the night. She needed a miracle, yet there wasn't a single thing that medical science could do for her. I took the healing Scriptures to her hospital room and spoke them out loud over her body. I said them hundreds of times. Within two hours, the monitors began to change. The nurses noticed an improvement in her breathing and her brain activity. By morning, she was sitting up in bed, fully alert and healed! The Bible says this about the Word of God:

> For the Word that God speaks is alive and full of power [making it active, operative, energizing, and effective]; it is sharper than any two-edged sword, penetrating to the dividing line of the breath of life (soul) and [the immortal] spirit, and of joints and marrow [of the deepest parts of our nature], exposing and sifting and analyzing and judging the very thoughts and purposes of the heart.   (Hebrews 4:12 AMP)

Many people don't receive the manifestations of their healings because they fail to recognize the power of God's

Word and fully esteem it in their lives. Some make the mistake of substituting personal prophecy for hearing God's Word. Others make the mistake of wanting their pastors, fellow church members, friends, or family members to sympathize with them or believe for them rather than attending to God's Word for themselves.

In other words, many people say they believe in healing, but they don't take God's medicine. They aren't taking it like they would take natural medicine—according to the directions.

When I was hospitalized, several people came and gave me personal prophecies about my future. A prophecy inspired by the Holy Spirit is a word of encouragement or edification from God given to one believer for another member (or a group of members) in the body of Christ. While this prophecy was a hope and encouragement to me, I was warned by my pastor, Randy Gilbert, to put prophecies on the shelf for the moment and to focus my attention on God's Word.

> *Many people say they believe in healing, but they don't take God's medicine like they would take natural medicine—according to the directions.*

At the time, I didn't fully understand his advice, but now I appreciate his wisdom. I've seen people literally stop believing God because someone else gave them a personal prophecy that they assumed would "automatically" come to pass. Even though a personal prophecy may be a legitimate encouragement from God, relying on it alone boils down to believing someone else's word over the written Word of God. While prophecy is good, it should never replace but only confirm God's Word in your heart.

> *All Scripture is God-breathed and is useful for teaching, rebuking, correcting and training in righteousness, so that the man of God may be thoroughly equipped for every good work.* (2 Timothy 3:16–17 NIV)

We are to test all words of prophecy to see if they are in keeping with God's Word. *"Do not quench the Spirit. Do not despise prophecies. Test all things; hold fast what is good"* (1 Thessalonians 5:19–21).

If God said it, you know it will surely come to pass. It is God's Word that, when embraced and acted upon, causes us to receive from Him. Therefore, keep taking in God's Word as medicine.

The Law of Displacement

If you have received a serious diagnosis, you must immerse yourself in God's Word.

Earlier, I wrote that when my body was sick, the Holy Spirit showed me a vision of two containers, one filled with dirty, muddy water, the other filled with crystal clear water. He told me that if I would take the container of clear water and pour it into the container of muddy water, it would be the same as taking His Word and pouring it into my body, which had been attacked by sickness. If I would continue to pour His Word in, it would displace or remove sickness from my body.

> **The Word of God will cleanse you and cause sickness to leave your body.**

When you immerse yourself in God's Word, it has a cleansing effect. It is the "washing of the water of the Word" (see Ephesians 5:26) that removes sickness and death and brings health and life. The Word of God will cleanse you and cause sickness to leave your body.

I've watched people diagnosed with fibromyalgia, carpal tunnel syndrome, eczema, autoimmune diseases, and other incurable diseases take God's Word like medicine and be cured.

Several years ago, Susan was diagnosed with cervical cancer. The doctor wrote on her medical file that she was in stage 3 or 4B—one of the final stages—of the disease. For three weeks, she immersed herself in God's Word. She attended to the healing promises and began to claim healing for her body. As she did, she started to feel stronger and more energized in her body. A few days later, she attended a series of healing meetings. The last night, she "believed she received" her healing. The same night, she hemorrhaged blood and had to be admitted to a local hospital and receive a blood transfusion. A CT scan on her cervix showed no evidence of the cancer. God had healed her, and she has been healed ever since!

My father had surgery to remove a blockage in his bile duct. As our family sat in the waiting room, the surgeon came in, gathered our family together, and shared the grim news. "I found a mass the size of my hand surrounding the main artery running through the pancreas. It was inoperable, and I am sorry to tell you that Mr. Wills has pancreatic cancer and about six months to live," he said. My brother-in-law, Ed, asked, "Doctor, how sure are you of your diagnosis?" The doctor said, "What do you mean?" Ed asked again, "How sure are you of your diagnosis—30 percent, 50 percent...100 percent?" The doctor replied, "I would say, 98 percent." Ed said, "Good. We will take the 2 percent because we believe in miracles and we serve a God of miracles!"

My father was discharged from the hospital and, for several months, daily immersed himself in healing Scriptures. He attended to God's Word. When he went back for a CT scan, it showed that his pancreas was clear and that he was healed! God's Word is medicine to all of our flesh.

> *For the word of God is alive and powerful.*
>
> (Hebrews 4:12 NLT)

One of the main ways God heals is by our appropriating what belongs to us through His Word. As you take time to attend to His Word through meditation and confession, God will illuminate His Word. You will discover that certain verses will begin to stand out more than others as they minister to you.

If you'll work the Word, the Word will work for you. God's Word is truth. It's the truth, the whole truth, and nothing but the truth.

Be Careful What You Hear

Jesus said,

> *Be careful what you are hearing. The measure [of thought and study] you give [to the truth you hear] will be the measure [of virtue and knowledge] that comes back to you—and more [besides] will be given to you who hear.*
>
> (Mark 4:24 AMP)

In other words, *"Be careful!"* means "Don't miss this!"

In Jesus' ministry, the multitudes came both to hear Jesus' words and to be healed. In that environment, the people put just as much importance on the hearing as the healing. To see the manifestation of our healing, we must do the same thing. If you want God's results, do what God says. Attend to His Word—incline your ear to His sayings, do not let His words depart from your eyes, and keep them in the midst of your heart. If you give His words your full and undivided attention, they will bring life, health, and medicine to all your flesh.

CHAPTER NINE

Step Three:
Understand the Significance of Words

"The tongue of the wise brings healing."
—Proverbs 12:18 (NIV)

Spoken words have the power to produce life or death, blessing or cursing. (See Proverbs 18:21.) If you're going to cooperate with God, you must understand that everything God does, He does with *words*. Every miracle in the Bible involved words. All of creation came into manifestation through words. The worlds were framed by the spoken word of God.

> *By faith we understand that the worlds were framed by the word of God, so that the things which are seen were not made of things which are visible.* (Hebrews 11:3)

There are some truths in the Bible that are good to know. There are others, however, that are *essential* to know—and one of them is how to receive your healing. If you don't know about healing, you might die young and never fulfill God's plan for your life. In order to understand healing, you must understand the significance of the words you speak.

Watch Your Words

Watch the words you speak. Be selective in choosing what you say and to whom you say it. The words you speak will either put you over or put you under. You cannot speak the problem and believe for your healing at the same time. *"If you claim to be religious but don't control your tongue, you are fooling yourself, and your religion is worthless"* (James 1:26 NLT).

Faith is simply agreeing with God. It's believing what He says about you and what He says you can have. For instance, Abram was given the promise that he would be the father of many nations. (See Genesis 12:1–3.) However, that didn't happen until Abram got in agreement with what God said about him and God eventually changed his name from Abram, "high father," to Abraham, "father of a multitude." (See Genesis 17:3–5.) Agreeing with God caused Abraham to grow strong in faith, and, like God, he called himself a father of many nations.

Furthermore, by coming into agreement with God, Abraham did not focus on the problem—his lack of a child. *"He did not consider his own body, already dead (since he was about a hundred years old), and the deadness of Sarah's womb"* (Romans 4:20). If you speak the problem, you will become problem-conscious. If you speak what God says, you will be God-conscious. All that's required for God to move in your life is agreement. He will not override your will; you must agree with Him.

Again, every miracle in the Bible involved words. If we want to cooperate with God, we must speak faith-filled words into the atmosphere. And we must believe that the words we speak will come to pass.

Marianne suffered from carpal tunnel syndrome for years. Despite repeated surgeries, nothing seemed to relieve her of the pain. I shared with her Isaiah 53, the great redemption chapter. I showed her where it said that Jesus bore her sickness and carried her pain. I asked her to meditate on that Scripture passage every day. For months, she mediated on Isaiah 53:4–5 and, as she did, the pain began to subside until, one day, she was healed. She then felt inspired to paint a beautiful painting depicting Isaiah 53 entitled "By His Stripes."

The Power of Words

How God Operates

We live in a natural world where most people are governed by their five physical senses, which do not discern the unseen spiritual realm. The system of the "world"—a way of thinking and its resultant actions that don't take God into account—is "death oriented." Many people have been programmed by this kind of thinking to speak negatively and to accept sickness as if it is their very own.

However, in the beginning, when God created the earth and everything in it, He used the method of speaking things into existence to bring change and life into this natural world. When God speaks, He always speaks the "end result."

I am God,...declaring the end from the beginning, and from ancient times the things that are not yet done, saying...
(Isaiah 46:9–10 KJV)

When God created human beings, He gave them authority and dominion over the natural world. Yet, when Jesus appeared on the earth, human beings weren't exercising their authority or dominion. People marveled at Jesus' authority. (See Matthew 7:28–29; Luke 4:36.) He spoke to water, and it turned into wine. He spoke to the wind, and it ceased to blow. He spoke to waves, and they calmed. He spoke to a withered hand, and it became whole. He spoke to fevers, and they disappeared. He spoke to a man who had been dead for four days, and the man walked out of his tomb alive. He spoke to a dead young man who was lying in a casket, and the young man sat up alive and was presented to his mother. (See, for example, John 2:1–11; Mark 4:35–41; Luke 6:6–10; Matthew 8:14–15; John 11:32–45; Luke 7:11–15.)

Jesus walked in an authority and dominion that no one else on earth exhibited. He is our example.

Years ago, a famous basketball player had a heart attack and died when he was only thirty-nine years of age. His collapse on the basketball court in a pick-up game was a shock to many people. What most of them didn't know was that, for years, he'd repeatedly said, "I'll never live to be forty years old."

That young man was the prophet of his own life. You are the prophet of yours.

Speak Your Miracle

To receive a miracle, you must speak words. Specifically, you must speak the *right* words. Your first words upon receiving a negative report can be the difference between life and death. Your words are like the rudder of a ship; they set the course of your life.

One of the first decisions my family and I made upon hearing my diagnosis was to guard the words we spoke. We decided to be very selective about the words we chose to use and with whom we chose to share information. We shared information only with close friends whom we knew would keep our situation confidential and who could stand in faith and agreement with us.

Step Three: Understand the Significance of Words

I was on a ward filled with patients who had incurable and terminal diseases. Sickness and death overwhelmed us. Everyone was frail, weak, and ill—and talking about their problems nonstop. They were consumed with their diagnoses, their pain, and the side effects of their medications. Amid all the hopelessness and despair, the Lord warned me, *Brian, if you allow yourself to think the same way and speak the same way as everyone else, you will get the same result.* Early on, I knew I had to guard my words.

The psychologists asked us daily, "How are you coping with the diagnosis?" Their goal was to get us to accept death and to reject any hope of healing. As I wrote earlier, they believed I was in denial and needed to accept the diagnosis and be prepared to make funeral arrangements. During each of these conversations, my family and I had to watch our words. With the doctor, we spoke to him on his terms but refused to accept any report contrary to God's report. If we had to share information with others, we told them what the doctor said but added, "However, we believe First Peter two, twenty-four, which says that by His stripes I am healed!" We refused to speak the problem or the diagnosis. We spoke only positive words of faith, life, and victory.

Another thing we did that seemed odd to most people was to speak to the cancer. Yet, Jesus said,

> *For assuredly, I say to you, whoever **says** to this mountain, "Be removed and be cast into the sea," and does not doubt in his heart, but believes that those things he **says** will be done, he will have whatever he **says**.*

> (Mark 11:23, emphasis added)

Words Move Mountains

Words move mountains. I would say out loud, "Cancer, in Jesus' name, I command you to go from my body. You have no right to my body. My body belongs to God. My body is God's property. So, I command you to die. You leave my body, in Jesus' name!"

That practice may sound strange, but remember that when Jesus walked the earth, He spoke to fevers, storms, evil spirits, and contrary circumstances. We are made in His image, and He instructed us to do the same. If you command sickness to leave your body, it must leave your body! Sickness must obey you. You have authority over sickness. Here is one of the Scriptures that reveal your power in Christ to heal the sick:

> *I tell you the truth, whatever you forbid on earth will be forbidden in heaven, and whatever you permit on earth will be permitted in heaven.* (Matthew 18:18 NLT)

When Rev. Norvel Hayes's daughter developed growths on her body, the Lord spoke to him and said, *How long are you going to put up with the growths on your daughter's body? You are the head of your house. If you will curse those growths in My name, they will die.* So, he commanded those growths to die and leave her body. After forty days, she was healed.

As I lay in the hospital on what the doctors called my deathbed, I began to say with my mouth, "I call my body healed. I call my body whole. I declare that my body functions according to the way God created it to function, and I forbid any malfunction, in Jesus' name." I spoke that way to the tumor that measured nine inches across my abdomen. I woke up one morning, and it had left my body!

Step Three: Understand the Significance of Words

One of my family members named Joyce had a blockage in her abdomen and was scheduled for exploratory surgery. I prayed for her the prayer of faith and commanded the blockage in her body to die, in Jesus' name. When she went in for surgery, the doctors were shocked to find a dead self-contained mass in her body weighing thirteen pounds! That was fifteen years ago, and she has been healed ever since. We have authority over sickness in Jesus' name.

You can't convince me there isn't power in the words we speak. The Bible says that God watches over His Word to perform it, so when we speak words that line up with His words, He will watch over and perform them.

Faith-Filled Words

The wisdom of the Bible has always said that we can have whatever we say based on God's will and Word, and medical science is finally beginning to get a glimmer of this truth. Research has revealed that the same part of your brain that controls your speech also controls your immune system. Cells respond when words are spoken!

This isn't the way doctors try to heal people; God chose this method. If you want to see circumstances change, speak faith-filled words into the atmosphere. Words are creative. They cause those things that are in the unseen realm to manifest in the seen realm. (See Hebrews 11:1.)

God works in such a way that He needs to hear your words. Look at this Scripture:

> *Words are creative. They cause those things that are in the unseen realm to manifest in the seen realm.*

10 Hours to Live

> *Death and life are in the power of the tongue, and those who*
> *love it will eat its fruit.*   (Proverbs 18:21)

Several years ago, Butch was diagnosed with cancer of the esophagus. His doctors told him the survival rate was only 5 percent. For the first time in his life, he heard the truth about healing and began to read healing Scriptures daily. He decided that no matter what, he would speak what God said. Each day, he would declare, "By Jesus' stripes I am healed. I am healed by Jesus' stripes." He refused to waver, despite monthly tests and visits with the doctor that revealed the cancer was still present. Then, one month, he went back for a CT scan. The doctor was shocked to find that there was no cancer in his body. Butch had "beaten the odds." He was healed!

I hope you're getting the picture. God wants to work in your life, but you have to get your words into agreement with His.

When the psychologists at the NIH asked if we had made funeral arrangements, I said, "No, I don't plan to die. Psalm 118:17 says, *'I shall not die, but live, and declare the works of the LORD.'* I am going to make it. I am going to live. I call my body healed. I call my body strong. I will fulfill my purpose." Although my words infuriated the psychologists, I didn't care. I knew that God, as well as a whole host of His heavenly angels, was listening, and *He* was whom I wanted to please.

Your Words Today Determine Your Future

Your life is a product of what you say. By coming into agreement with God and saying what God says, you can have what He says you can have! "Do I really have to say it?"

someone may ask. Yes! God said, *"By your words you will be justified, and by your words you will be condemned"* (Matthew 12:37).

Have no doubt about it; your words today determine your future tomorrow.

Christianity has been called "The Great Confession." Words are powerful. Words are creative. Choose to speak God's Word and watch your mountains move out of the way.

CHAPTER TEN

Step Four:

Know That Healing Was Purchased on Calvary

"Surely He has borne our griefs (sicknesses, weaknesses, and distresses) and carried our sorrows and pains [of punishment]."
—Isaiah 53:4 (AMP)

You must have the right perspective in order to receive from God. Too often, people are waiting for God to heal them when, in reality, He already has done so. Religion has taught us that healing either was part of a past work or is a future blessing for when we get to heaven one day. However, healing is for *today.*

Redeemed from the Entire Curse

In order to grasp this revelation that healing is for today, you must understand that Jesus redeemed us from the *entire* curse.

Christ has redeemed us from the curse..., that the blessing of Abraham might come upon the Gentiles in Christ Jesus.
(Galatians 3:13–14)

God has already done everything He is going to do in purchasing our redemption. First Peter 2:24 tells us that by Jesus' stripes, we *were* healed. Christ has redeemed us from the curse. The curse includes spiritual death, sickness, and poverty. The price has been paid in full. That's the good news of the gospel!

Again, most Christians are waiting on God for their healing. They say, "I'm just waiting on the Lord. If He wants to heal me, He will." What they don't realize is that Jesus purchased their healing on Calvary two thousand years ago. They are waiting on God; meanwhile, He is waiting on *them*.

We don't hear believers say, "I'm just waiting on God to save me." The truth is that God already has saved us. Salvation is a free gift, and it's up to us to receive it. We don't receive it by works. (See Ephesians 2:8–9.) Like salvation, healing is a redemptive blessing that we receive by faith. The same type of faith through which you were saved is the faith through which you will receive your healing. You just have to believe in the saving work that Jesus did for you on the cross.

Faith Is Now

> **No matter what your symptoms, look back to Calvary and say, "By Jesus' stripes I was healed."**

Faith is now. No matter what your symptoms, don't look forward to the day when God will heal you. Look back to Calvary and say, "By Jesus' stripes I *was* healed." If you have the mind-set that you must wait on God for your healing, then you'll be waiting for a long time, and, most likely, you will never receive it.

Again, you must see things from the right perspective—a perspective that looks back on what has already been done by Jesus. The apostle Paul prayed for the church,

...that the God of our Lord Jesus Christ, the Father of glory, may give to you the spirit of wisdom and revelation in the knowledge of Him, the eyes of your understanding being enlightened; that you may know what is the hope of His calling, what are the riches of the glory of His inheritance in the saints. (Ephesians 1:17–18)

We need a personal revelation of what Jesus purchased for us on Calvary and of the glorious inheritance that is ours through Jesus Christ!

Healing Is the Children's Bread

In Matthew 15, there is the story of a woman from Canaan who came to Jesus because she wanted healing and deliverance for her daughter, who was *"severely demon-possessed"* (verse 22). Let's get this story straight. This woman wasn't a pillar in the church. She wasn't in covenant with God; she was a "heathen." Jesus answered her by saying, *"It is not good to take the children's bread and throw it to the little dogs"* (verse 26).

I want to focus on the phrase *"the children's bread,"* because it is significant to our understanding of our inheritance in Jesus Christ. However, I also want to point out that this woman persevered and did receive healing for her daughter, even though she was outside the covenant, because of her strong faith in Jesus and what He could do for her.

And she said, "Yes, Lord, yet even the little dogs eat the crumbs which fall from their masters' table." Then Jesus answered and said to her, "O woman, great is your faith! Let it be to you as you desire." And her daughter was healed from that very hour. (Matthew 15:27–28)

God's children are those who are in covenant with Him. Notice that Jesus referred to healing as *"the children's bread."* In other words, He said that healing belongs to God's children. Covenant with God was made available to all people through the sacrifice of Jesus Christ. Do you get that? Healing belongs to you!

Jesus' death on the cross was a work of substitution. (See, for example, Romans 5:8–10; 1 Thessalonians 5:9–10.) He took our place. He paid the price for sin as well as for sickness. On the cross, God the Father laid upon Jesus all the sins of the world. At the whipping post where He was scourged, God the Father laid upon Jesus all the sickness of the world. That means Jesus has already borne the sickness that the devil is trying to put on you. Don't accept it!

For seven years, Margie suffered with hemorrhoids. Despite various surgeries and doctor's visits, she could not seem to get better; in fact, her condition only got worse. When she heard about healing, she began to mediate on God's promises. One day, while she was meditating on Isaiah 53:4 in her kitchen, the Holy Spirit illuminated to her the word *"surely"*: *"Surely He has borne our griefs (sicknesses, weaknesses, and distresses) and carried our sorrows and pains [of punishment]"* (AMP). She thought to herself, "Surely means surely." Then, she said out loud, "Surely means surely." She walked around her kitchen proclaiming, "Surely Jesus bore my sickness and carried my pains!" At that moment, she realized that if Jesus had borne her sickness for her, then she should not have to bear it. A change came over her body, and she was healed at that very moment!

The Whole Package

When I was given a death sentence by the doctors, I realized that medical science offered no hope, but Jesus did.

As I listened to the doctors saying that my diagnosis was incurable and terminal, I realized that God was the only One who could offer hope and give me new life. I discovered for myself the good news about salvation.

You see, salvation is a whole package. It includes both forgiveness and healing. When Jesus walked the earth, the Pharisees became used to His healing people, but they were offended when He claimed to forgive sins! (See, for example, Luke 5:17–25.)

Salvation includes both forgiveness and healing.

In the New Testament, the Greek word *sozo* means "to save" or "to heal." These meanings are sometimes used interchangeably. Remember the case of the woman with the twelve-year, chronic flow of blood who touched the hem of Jesus' clothing for healing? *"Jesus turned around, and when He saw her He said, 'Be of good cheer, daughter; your faith has made you well ["made thee whole" KJV; "healed you" NIV]'"* (Matthew 9:22). The Greek word that is translated *"made you well"* is *sozo.*

Jesus preached the gospel of spiritual salvation and physical healing. The early church preached the same gospel. That's the gospel we are called to preach and to live today.

You can't receive what you haven't been taught. When you teach and preach salvation, people receive salvation. When you teach and preach healing, people receive healing.

I received Jesus as my Lord and Savior at a young age. However, as I lay in the hospital fighting for my life, I accepted Christ as my Healer. I realized that I was not trying to get healed as much as I was *already healed.* How, you may wonder, could I think I was already healed when the doctors were predicting my immediate demise? It's because I knew that God's Word is truth, and truth always trumps fact. The facts were that I'd been diagnosed with Burkitt's lymphoma and that medical science had no cure. However, God said, *"By* [Jesus'] *stripes you were healed"* (1 Peter 2:24). The Bible says that we *were* healed, which, again, is in the past tense. If we *were healed,* then we *are healed.* That was the truth of my situation.

In Psalm 103, we are reminded not to forget our covenant benefits. David listed some of those benefits of salvation:

> *Bless the LORD, O my soul, and all that is within me, bless His holy name. Bless the LORD, O my soul, and forget none of His benefits; who pardons all your iniquities, who heals all your diseases; who redeems your life from the pit, who crowns you with lovingkindness and compassion; who satisfies your years with good things, so that your youth is renewed like the eagle.* (verses 1–5 NASB)

That is an amazing list of benefits! And yet, so many people have forgotten that God gave them to us. Our society has become conditioned to accept sickness. As I watched others cope with cancer at the NIH, I saw them become so consumed with their disease that it overwhelmed any realization they had of God's benefits package.

Now that I've been in ministry for over twenty years, I've learned some additional aspects to healing. A big part of the healing ministry is talking people out of their problems. Many of them are ignorant of what Jesus purchased for them on the cross. Some, however, would rather hold on to their sicknesses than accept healing. They may not want to exercise the faith needed for God to heal them, they may want people to keep feeling sorry for them because of their illnesses, or they may have some other reason.

The greatest insult you can give God is to discredit His Son's sacrifice and refuse the freedom He purchased for you. Jesus did not suffer for us so that we could hold on to sickness. We owe it to God to do all we can to receive His redemptive benefits. If we choose to accept sickness, then Jesus' sacrifice at the whipping post was in vain.

If you challenge nothing, you change nothing. Healing belongs to you. It is a redemptive blessing and a benefit provided for every believer.

> *Healing belongs to you. It is a redemptive blessing and a benefit provided for every believer.*

The entire gospel hinges on the covenantal relationship between God and the human beings that He created, loved, and redeemed through His Son Jesus Christ. The New Testament unfolds the fulfillment of God's plan of redemption through the new covenant.

The more you understand the power and authority delegated to you by God through this covenant, the less likely you will be to waver in your faith for healing.

A Wonderful New Covenant in Christ

You may think you're not worthy for God to heal and protect you, but that's the world's way of thinking. Take a good look at what God says about you and me:

> *But you are a chosen race, a royal priesthood, a holy nation, a people for God's own possession, so that you may proclaim the excellencies of Him who has called you out of darkness into His marvelous light; for you once were not a people, but*

now you are the people of God; you had not received mercy, but now you have received mercy.   (1 Peter 2:9–10 NASB)

Jesus Christ [is] the faithful witness, the firstborn from the dead, and the ruler over the kings of the earth. [He] who loved us and washed us from our sins in His own blood, and has made us kings and priests to His God and Father.

(Revelation 1:5–6)

This is who God says you are, and all the resources of heaven are behind you to enable you to live in the reality of your new position in Christ. All you have to do is believe.

Communion Releases Blessings

Jesus spoke about the new covenant to His disciples the night before His crucifixion. This covenant is symbolized by Communion, or the Lord's Table. Joining them for the Last Supper, Jesus said, *"I have earnestly desired to eat this Passover with you before I suffer"* (Luke 22:15 NASB).

As they were eating, Jesus took bread, blessed and broke it, and gave it to the disciples and said, "Take, eat; this is My body." Then He took the cup, and gave thanks, and gave it to them, saying, "Drink from it, all of you. For this is My blood of the new covenant, which is shed for many for the remission of sins."   (Matthew 26:26–28)

In the same manner [Jesus] also took the cup after supper, saying, "This cup is the new covenant in My blood. This do, as often as you drink it, in remembrance of Me."

(1 Corinthians 11:25)

I believe the act of taking Communion in faith is not just a ritual; it connects us to our covenant with God through

Jesus Christ and releases spiritual strength and the blessings of God in our lives, and that's why I took Communion on a regular basis in the hospital. Paul instructed the church at Corinth to observe the Lord's Table. (See 1 Corinthians 11:23–26.) Yet, he told them that many were weak, sick, and dying prematurely because they were not putting their faith in the *"Lord's body"* (verse 29) for spiritual renewal and healing during Communion but were apparently selfishly hurrying to eat as much as they could of the meal before others arrived. Paul also said we are to "judge ourselves" before taking communion. We should examine our hearts to see if we are harboring any unforgiveness or have other sins in our lives that we need to repent of and ask forgiveness for.

> *Therefore, whoever eats the bread or drinks the cup of the Lord in an unworthy manner will be guilty of sinning against the body and blood of the Lord. A man ought to examine himself before he eats of the bread and drinks of the cup. For anyone who eats and drinks without recognizing the body of the Lord eats and drinks judgment on himself. That is why many among you are weak and sick, and a number of you have fallen asleep. But if we judged ourselves, we would not come under judgment. When we are judged by the Lord, we are being disciplined so that we will not be condemned with the world. So then, my brothers, when you come together to eat, wait for each other. If anyone is hungry, he should eat at home, so that when you meet together it may not result in judgment.* (1 Corinthians 11:27–34 NIV)

Communion should be a time to reverently reflect on Christ's atoning work on the cross for us and to seek the Lord for whatever we need in our lives, including healing. What if, instead of laying out their weekly laundry lists of people to pray for who are sick, churches today began to conduct Communion and healing services, releasing blessings into their congregations?

Pastor John was an Episcopal priest who was dying of cancer and given six months to live. When he saw he could receive healing through Communion, he began to take the sacrament on a daily basis. Months later, he called me to tell me he was healed!

My wife, Beth, went to a dermatologist because she had a dark brown spot the size of a quarter on her foot. The doctor tried to scrape it off. He was very concerned and told her further tests would have to be done. That night, we took Communion; days later, the spot was gone!

You can take Communion by yourself in your home. You don't have to wait for a priest or a minister. You can take it daily. Actually, the more often you take it, the more real it becomes to you and the more power is released to you. Taking Communion is one way we appropriate what belongs to us. When we place our faith in the finished work of Jesus, we receive the benefits of that work. We receive forgiveness *and* healing.

CHAPTER ELEVEN

Step Five:
Listen and Obey

"The spirit of a man is the lamp of the LORD, searching all the inner depths of his heart."
—Proverbs 20:27

Each person is unique, and every situation is different. However, healing always begins on the inside—in our hearts. With our hearts, we receive from God. Things happen first on the inside, and then they manifest on the outside. This is similar to the process of salvation. *"For with the heart one believes unto righteousness, and with the mouth confession is made unto salvation"* (Romans 10:10).

When I first cried out to the Lord for healing, I told Him that if He would heal me, I would do whatever He wanted me to do. I heard a voice on the inside say, *Son, I am your Healer, and I will manifest healing to you as you take the steps I tell you to take. You will walk through the fire and not be burned.*

That's when I realized I had a part to play in my healing.

God Plays a Part, and We Play a Part

Some people put all the responsibility for healing on God. But, with any miracle, there is always a part that God plays and a part that man plays. In Jesus' ministry, He often gave people steps to take in regard to their healing. He told the ten lepers to go and show themselves to the priests. (See Luke 17:11–14.) He told the blind man to go and wash in the pool of Siloam. (See John 9:1–7.) He told the man with the withered hand to stretch out his hand. (See, for example, Matthew 12:9–13.) Their obedience became a catalyst to release the miraculous.

Your ability to listen to your heart and be led by the Holy Spirit is a vital key to receiving from God. As with those who were healed in the Bible, your obedience is a catalyst to release the miraculous in your life.

Jesus performed His first miracle at a wedding when the host family ran out of wine. His mother, Mary, said to the servants, in effect, "Whatever He tells you to do, do it." (See John 2:1–11.) Similarly, the key to every miracle is to follow those simple instructions: "Whatever He tells you to do, do it."

The Leading and Guidance of the Holy Spirit

How do we do whatever God tells us to do? The Holy Spirit is our Helper. He has been sent to lead us and guide us. (See, for example, John 14:26; 16:13.) I have often heard Rev. Keith Moore say, "If you look to the Holy Spirit, He will lead you out of sickness into healing, out of defeat into victory, every time."

The Holy Spirit is a real Person. As you yield to Him and draw on His strength, He can become more real to you than the clothes you wear, the car you drive, and the house where you live.

Countless times, the Holy Spirit has led my family and me in ministry, in business, and in our personal lives. In college, I injured my lower back and right hip. I went to a chiropractor. I took deep heat treatments to relieve the pain. One day, as I began to seek the Lord about it, the Holy

Spirit showed me a spiritual picture of my going to a healing service and having a certain healing minister pray for me. Later, I looked up the ministry itinerary and discovered that that particular minister would be within driving distance in less than two months. Then, the Holy Spirit said to me, *Open your Bible, find healing Scriptures that cover your case, and meditate on those Scriptures until it is time for you to attend the service and get prayed for to be healed.*

I obeyed those instructions. My college friends had watched me suffer and struggle with pain for weeks. I told them that I was going to a healing service and would come back totally healed. Weeks later, when I went to the service, I was instantly healed. What a testimony it was to my friends when I went back to college.

One pastor had been experiencing migraine headaches and couldn't seem to get rid of them, so he spent time praying in the Spirit. One day, the Holy Spirit told him He was drinking too much coffee and that if he could cut back his consumption, his headaches would cease. He did, and they did. Thank God for the Holy Spirit!

No two situations are just alike, but the Holy Spirit knows the key to each one of them. He sees what may not show up on a medical X-ray. It doesn't matter if the cause is natural, spiritual, or chemical. The Holy Spirit sees, knows, and has the solution. All we need to do is hear from Him.

Some people try to come up with formulas for receiving healing. For instance, they may say that each sickness has a specific root cause. The Bible, however, doesn't tell us to focus on root causes. Rather, we are directed to put the emphasis on the leading and guidance of the Holy Spirit. Jesus dealt with sickness through the power of the Holy Spirit, and we should deal with sickness in the same way.

One reason why people are attacked with illness is simply that we live in a sin-perverted universe. Sickness and death are working in this world, and that's why we must resist them. As Christians, we are not immune to problems, but we can always be victorious over them.

In Christ, we are under a new spiritual law. The Bible says that the law of the Spirit of life has set us free from the law of sin and death. (See Romans 8:2.)

Take Time to Hear God's Voice

For as many as are led by the Spirit of God, these are sons of God. (Romans 8:14)

If you are having difficulty hearing God's voice, take time to get alone with Him. In the early church, the people ministered to the Lord, and then the Holy Spirit ministered back to them. The Holy Spirit gave them the wisdom and instruction they needed.

As they ministered to the Lord and fasted, the Holy Spirit said,.... (Acts 13:2)

"Ministering to the Lord" means spending time in His presence. When you spend time with the Lord, tell Him how much you love Him, thanking Him for all the things He has done for you and extolling Him for who He is.

As you minister to the Lord, the Lord will have something to say. He will lead you and guide you by His Spirit. You don't have to be fearful or concerned about your situation because God will give you direction and *"tell you things to come"* (John 16:13.)

How does the Holy Spirit lead us?

He leads us to open the Bible so that He may reveal the truth to us through His written Word. He also leads us through the *"still small voice"* (1 Kings 19:12), or the inward voice, and the voice of our conscience. He will lead us through the "inward witness" in our hearts, which is like a green light or red light on the inside. It is a gentle prompting or peace that assures that something is right for us to do or that it is all right for us not to take a certain action; likewise, it is a prompting or a lack of peace about something we are not supposed to do or something we are meant to do but have left undone.

Obey What He Tells You

Extend Forgiveness

You may remember that the first step the Lord showed me in regard to my healing was to address the unforgiveness that I had. When I confessed it and dealt with it, it felt like a huge burden had been lifted off my shoulders. When I forgave, my kidneys actually began to function again.

To hold unforgiveness and offenses in your heart is a sin, and that sin will block your healing the way it blocked mine until the Lord revealed it to me. Perhaps one of the more sobering Scriptures regarding forgiveness is found in Mark 11:25: *"And when you stand praying, if you hold anything against anyone, forgive him, so that your Father in heaven may forgive you your sins"* (NIV).

Ask the Holy Spirit to Reveal Any Hindrances

If you want your faith to work, you must continually walk in a loving relationship with others and stay in fellowship with God. Ask the Holy Spirit to reveal anything that could be a hindrance. Repent of any sin. Get your heart right with God.

Sometimes, people haven't yet received their healings because they are missing the mark in some way. Maybe it has to do with not spending time with the Lord or not doing something He instructed them to do. I've seen people healed as they were prompted to right a wrong or to tithe or give. In my case, the second step the Lord showed me in regard to my healing was to tithe. Tithing—giving 10 percent of our income to the Lord's work—connects us with our covenant and allows God's blessings to flow in our lives. (See, for example, Malachi 3:8–11.)

Make Changes

> *It has been proven that many of those who survive serious and life-threatening illnesses are those who are willing to make lifestyle changes.*

It has been proven that many of those who survive serious and life-threatening illnesses are those who are willing to make lifestyle changes. These could be natural changes or spiritual changes. Sometimes, people need to make alterations in diet or exercise.

Often, the Holy Spirit has been prompting us to do something different, but we've resisted His leading. He will remind us of things He has spoken to us about before. The way God leads you in regard to change may seem irrelevant to what you are going through, but don't let that stop you. Whatever He says, do it.

When I was in the hospital, I was several hours from home in a different city and state. Our family didn't have church friends or people calling us all the time to encourage us. We were removed from the natural comforts of home, but that was when we learned to rely on the Holy Spirit—the Greater One living inside of us. Every day, we looked to Him to guide us and strengthen us. He was our constant Helper and Companion.

The Holy Spirit knows the key to your situation. He has a plan and a strategy to lead you out of sickness and into healing. If you're not sure what to do, ask God for wisdom.

> *If any of you lacks wisdom, let him ask of God, who gives to all liberally and without reproach, and it will be given to him.* (James 1:5)

Expect Him to show you steps to take! Your obedience will be a catalyst to release God's blessings.

Likewise, when making decisions concerning treatments and procedures, follow the Holy Spirit's inward leading. You may have to process information and circumstances through your intellect, but, in the end, follow your heart. Take time to get alone with God. Get your mind quiet and follow the peace He gives you. Then, you will go out with joy and be led forth with peace. (See Isaiah 55:12.)

CHAPTER TWELVE

Step Six:
<u>Win the Battle</u>

"For our struggle is not against flesh and blood, but against the rulers, against the authorities, against the powers of this dark world and against the spiritual forces of evil in the heavenly realms."
—Ephesians 6:12 (NIV)

In the New Testament, we are often reminded of the spiritual battle we are fighting. We are told to put on the *"whole armor of God"* (Ephesians 6:13), *"fight the good fight of faith"* (1 Timothy 6:12), and resist the enemy (see James 4:7; 1 Peter 5:8–9). In any war, it's important to know the enemy. Our enemy, Satan, is *"the god of this world"* (2 Corinthians 4:4 KJV). He comes to steal, kill, and destroy. (See John 10:10.) He tries to keep the Word of God from being sown in your heart. (See Matthew 13:19; Luke 8:11–12.) When you face a physical attack, the major ways he attempts to sabotage your faith are through fear, distractions, and discouragement.

Four Things to Know about Your Battle

So many times, people don't know whether God or the devil is behind the negative things that are happening in their lives. This is because they don't know God's true nature of love and goodness or the certainty of Satan and his evil work in this world.

Very often, people say about their illnesses, "God is in control." But God is not the author of, nor is He responsible for, the bad things that happen here on the earth. John Alexander Dowie said, "Disease [is] the foul offspring of its father, Satan and its mother, Sin."[2] When Adam sinned after listening to Satan's lies, sickness and death entered the world.

There are four things you need to know about your battle with sickness:

1. You have an enemy. *"Be sober, be vigilant; because your adversary the devil walks about like a roaring lion, seeking whom he may devour"* (1 Peter 5:8).

2. You are in a spiritual battle. *"For though we walk in the flesh, we do not war according to the flesh. For the weapons of our warfare are not carnal but mighty in God for pulling down strongholds"* (2 Corinthians 10:3–4).

3. Satan has a plan. *"The thief does not come except to steal, and to kill, and to destroy"* (John 10:10).

4. God has a greater plan through Jesus Christ. *"I have come that they may have life, and that they may have it more abundantly"* (John 10:10).

> **The way to override Satan's work is to pray to the heavenly Father in faith and to speak the Word of God in faith.**

Through the Lord's Prayer, Jesus taught His disciples how to pray. He instructed them to pray, *"Your will be done on earth as it is in heaven"* (Matthew 6:10; Luke 11:2). If God is "in control," in the sense that everything that happens should just be accepted, why would Jesus tell them to pray in that way? It is because God's will is not being done on the earth. Satan is the god

---

[2] Charles A. Jennings, comp., "Life & Ministry of John Alexander Dowie," www.truthinhistory.org/life-ministry-of-john-alexander-dowie.html.

of this world. The way to override Satan's work is to pray to the heavenly Father in faith and to speak the Word of God in faith. God wants us to partner with Him in spreading His kingdom and will on earth.

Replace Fear with Faith

Anyone who has ever been given a bad diagnosis has had to deal with fear. The enemy will try to paralyze you with fear. For the first fifteen days of my hospitalization, I didn't battle cancer as much as I fought fear.

To counteract the enemy's sabotage of your faith, and therefore your healing, you will first need to rebuke fear. There are times when you must exercise your spiritual authority over the enemy. You may need to tell Satan to take his hands off your body. However, don't spend the majority of your time giving attention to the devil. Rather, place greater attention on the truth of God's Word, because it is the truth that will set you free. (See John 8:32 NIV.)

The Bible says, *"For God has not given us a spirit of fear, but of power and of love and of a sound mind"* (2 Timothy 1:7). Fear is an open door for the enemy to work. It is like a magnet that draws bad things into our lives. Fear also brings torment. (See 1 John 4:18.)

During the fifteen days that I battled fear, I didn't want to fall asleep. Fearful thoughts bombarded my mind. *You have cancer. You have an incurable disease. You are not going to live much longer.* Not only that, but my physical body seemed to agree. I suffered intense pain as the tumor grew by the hour. The nurses used a measuring tape to monitor the growth of the mushrooming tumor in my abdomen. Over and over again, the enemy downloaded scenes of my own funeral into my mind. I knew that if I didn't conquer the fear, I would never conquer cancer.

When fear comes, you can't curl up into a fetal position and play dead. You must combat fear with words. Regardless of how you feel, you must open your mouth and speak faith-filled words. At night, in particular, fear tried to overwhelm me. I tossed and turned in my bed, unable to find rest. Finally, I would sit up, turn on the light, and recite the healing promises.

> *Just because you battle occasional thoughts of doubt or fear doesn't mean you're not in faith.*

"Fear, I resist you in Jesus' name," I would say. "God has not given me a spirit of fear but of power, love, and a sound mind. God's Word says I'm healed, so I'm healed. I will live and not die. I will declare the works of the Lord. By Jesus' stripes, I was healed, and if I *was* healed, then I *am* healed."

I would say these truths until the peace of God settled over my mind and heart.

> *You will keep in perfect peace all who trust in you, all whose thoughts are fixed on you!* (Isaiah 26:3 NLT)

Just because you battle occasional thoughts of doubt or fear doesn't mean you're not in faith. Rev. Kenneth E. Hagin used to say, "Just because the birds fly over your head doesn't mean you have to let them nest in your hair." You must resist those thoughts, and they will flee from you. (See James 4:7.)

Replace Distractions with a Focus on God's Word

Positive Words Override Negative Thoughts

Fighting the good fight of faith involves staying focused on the Word of God and not becoming distracted. Distractions are a tool of the enemy to get you off course.

I once ministered to a man who'd been diagnosed with lung cancer and given six months to live. He was only forty years old, and he said, "I don't want my social life to change in order to spend time in Scripture all day." The two times I visited him in his home, I realized that he'd put his social life above his healing. There were so many people stopping by to visit that it was futile trying to minister the Word to him. He didn't make time for it.

Your life will go in the direction of your most dominant thoughts. If negative thoughts are bombarding you, interrupt them by speaking positive words. Words dominate thoughts. When Jesus was being tempted by Satan in the wilderness, He resisted by saying, *"It is written…."* (See, for example, Matthew 4:4, 7, 10.)

> *Your life will go in the direction of your most dominant thoughts.*

What kinds of thoughts are you having? The real battle for your life is fought over your mind. The Bible tells us that we are to cast down and take captive every thought that is not in agreement with God's Word.

> *Casting down imaginations and every high thing that exalts itself against the knowledge of God, bringing every thought into captivity to the obedience of Christ.*
>
> (2 Corinthians 10:5)

Never allow a mental picture of failure to remain in your mind. Keep your mind on the answer rather than the problem. Satan can move in the suggestion realm; not every thought, feeling, dream, or imagination comes from God. Satan can insert a thought or an idea. Anything that doesn't build you up or bring peace is from the devil and needs to be cast down and replaced with truth.

The story in the Bible of Jairus, a synagogue ruler, is a good example. Jairus's daughter was at the point of death when he asked Jesus to heal her. When news arrived from Jairus's house that his daughter had already died, Jesus said, *"Do not be afraid; only believe"* (Mark 5:36; Luke 8:50). Jesus didn't want a mental picture of failure to remain in Jairus's mind.

Doubt your doubts and feed your faith.

Persistence Pays Off

I heard a definition of *persist* that is very appropriate to winning your battle: "to apply constant, nonstop, continued, relentless pressure until all resistance is broken and the desired result is obtained."

Persistence pays off. You must become more persistent with God's Word than the enemy is in bombarding you with thoughts of defeat and failure.

Medical researchers studied the qualities of patients who experienced a spontaneous healing. The first quality of those who beat impossible odds was that they refused to take no for an answer. They refused to quit. They took the initiative for their healing.

Similarly, in Jesus' ministry, those who received healing were those who were persistent. Four men carried a paralyzed friend on a pallet to a meeting in a home where Jesus was teaching. The house was packed with people, so there was no room to get inside, and yet these men persisted and let their friend down into the room through the roof. Jesus healed the man. *"When Jesus saw their faith, He said to the paralytic, 'Son, your sins are forgiven you....I say to you, arise, take up your bed, and go to your house'"* (Mark 2:5, 11). We see that same kind of persistence in the two blind men (see Matthew 9:27–30;

20:30–34), in blind Bartimaeus (see Mark 10:46–52), and the woman with the chronic flow of blood (see, for example, Luke 8:43–48). Each of them was healed.

Don't have a predetermined idea of how you think your healing will manifest.

I've witnessed countless people who have refused ministry when the power of God was present to heal. They said they didn't need to receive ministry because they already knew how their healing would manifest. That's a trap. Years later, most of them still struggled with sickness.

Remember the story of Naaman the leper? He came from Syria to the prophet Elisha's house, only to have Elisha's servant come to the door and tell him to go wash in the Jordan River seven times. Naaman almost missed his healing because he was certain how it would come about. He said, *"Indeed, I said to myself, 'He will surely come out to me, and stand and call on the name of the LORD his God, and wave his hand over the place, and heal the leprosy'"* (2 Kings 5:11). When he accepted the prophet's message and did what Elisha told him to do, he was healed.

Don't set deadlines.

You can't put your faith in time frames; put your faith only in God's Word. The enemy will try to sabotage your faith by using time against you. Your faith is rooted and grounded in God's Word, and you are in it for the long term if that's what it takes.

Believe God's report over any other report.

God's power is released to those who believe His Word above any other report. Don't consider the doctor's report or how your body feels or looks. God's Word is your only answer. It must be your Final Answer.

Keep your spirit strong.

Proverbs 18:14 says, *"The strong spirit of a man sustains him in bodily pain or trouble, but a weak and broken spirit who can raise up or bear?"* (AMP). Keep your spirit strong by feeding it with the Word of God and exercising it through prayer, praise, and praying in the Spirit. (See Ephesians 6:18.)

Replace Discouragement with Strength from God

If you've stood in prayer for any length of time, you've probably faced discouragement. Discouragement is a tactic of the enemy to get you to give up and quit. Discouragement comes when things don't manifest in the way you thought they would or as quickly as you thought they would. *"Hope deferred makes the heart sick, but when the desire comes, it is a tree of life"* (Proverbs 13:12).

The enemy's strategy is to wear you down and wear you out. He hopes to deter your faith. He uses the passing of time to whisper that maybe it's not God's will to heal you. He uses it to tell you that you don't have enough faith. These are lies and traps of the enemy. Don't let yourself fall for them.

For months in the hospital, I battled fear, infections, fatigue, and weariness. During one battle, I suffered not only infection, but also a compromised immune system and a very high fever. The doctors thought the candida would spread to my heart and that I would be dead within a few hours. My body felt like it was on fire. To reduce the risk of my fever spiking any higher, the nurses rubbed oil into my skin. The intense battle lasted night and day for three weeks. I felt like my faith was being tested past its limits. At the end, I felt like a prize fighter who had endured the fight of his life and was still standing in the final round.

I told the devil that he was going to regret ever attacking me. I explained that when I got out of the hospital, I would travel the world and tell others about the goodness of God and the saving knowledge of Jesus Christ. I remembered the *rhema* words I had received—specific words that the Holy Spirit had spoken to me—and spent time praying in the Spirit, which built me up and gave me new strength. Then, I faced my next battle with renewed strength and vision.

Don't Give Up!

The Bible tells us, *"Do not become sluggish, but imitate those who through faith and patience inherit the promises"* (Hebrews 6:12). The Greek word translated *"patience"* might also be translated as *perseverance*. Faith is persistent; it is tenacious.

In an earlier chapter, I briefly mentioned the Canaanite woman who came to Jesus asking that He heal and deliver her demon-possessed daughter. (See Matthew 15:22–28.) The Scripture says that after she came to Him and cried out for mercy, *"He answered her not a word"* (verse 23).

Have you ever prayed and felt like God wasn't listening to or answering your prayer? If this scenario, in which Jesus didn't answer the woman's request right away, happened today, a lot of people would say, "Well, I guess it's not God's will for her daughter to be healed." They would be wrong, because God's will had nothing to do with it.

What did the woman do? She didn't get offended, and she didn't quit. She refused to give up. She persevered. She was persistent. In the end, Jesus healed her daughter. *"Then Jesus answered and said to her, 'O woman, great is your faith! Let it be to you as you desire.' And her daughter was healed from that very hour"* (verse 28). It takes bulldog faith and absolute persistence to obtain God's promises.

We're in a spiritual battle. To win, we must use God's Word. We must pick up our spiritual weapons. We must be more persistent than the enemy. I've seen some of the greatest miracles occur at the midnight hour when things looked hopeless. One man said, "Devil, you might as well give up, because I don't plan to!"

> *Faith refuses to quit. Don't give up, because God will see you through.*

Faith refuses to quit. Don't quit. Don't give up, because God will see you through. As Winston Churchill famously said, "Never, never, never give up."

CHAPTER THIRTEEN

Step Seven:
Create an Atmosphere for God

"Those who live in the shelter of the Most High will find
rest in the shadow of the Almighty."
—Psalm 91:1 (NLT)

Whatever atmosphere you create will determine what is manifest in your life. You can create an atmosphere for God to move. Or, you can create an atmosphere in which the enemy reigns. For instance, if you allow your home to be filled with negativity, discord, and oppression, it will be difficult to stand in faith, so you must learn to counteract such influences when they come against you.

You may remember the movie *Field of Dreams*. It's the story of an Iowa corn farmer who heard a voice in his cornfield say, "If you build it, they will come." He interpreted the message as an instruction to build a baseball field on his farm. Despite his misgivings, he built the field—and the baseball players came.

If you build an atmosphere for God to move, He will come.

The thirteenth floor of the NIH hospital was filled with those who had incurable and terminal illnesses. Sickness, fear, hopelessness, and despair permeated the atmosphere as cancer patients tried to survive the deadly treatments and their side effects. The news spread fast when one of our comrades died, and the nurses were all too eager to tell us about it. This news always left an even more sobering tone on a ward filled with death.

During my ordeal, my mother read Psalm 91 aloud several times each day. Like many promises in the Bible, it starts with a condition:

> *He who dwells in the secret place of the Most High shall abide under the shadow of the Almighty.*   (Psalm 91:1)

And it ends with a promise:

> *Because he has set his love upon Me, therefore I will deliver him; I will set him on high, because he has known My name. He shall call upon Me, and I will answer him; I will be with him in trouble; I will deliver him and honor him. With long life I will satisfy him, and show him My salvation.*
>
> (verses 14–16)

The Secret Place

There is a *"secret place"* where God dwells. We sought to abide and dwell in that place, and to create the atmosphere for Him to dwell. As my friends died, the enemy tried to fill our minds with doubt and our hearts with grief. I fought back by declaring, "A thousand may fall at our side and ten thousand at our right hand, but it shall not come near me." (See Psalm 91:7.)

Early on, we set parameters. Again, we were very selective about what we spoke and how we spent our time. We knew we were in a battle and that every moment meant the difference between life and death. We didn't watch television like other patients and their families. For months, we were unaware of anything that went on in the outside world. Like soldiers on the battlefield, we were engaged in spiritual warfare every day. We had close friends whom we called on occasion, but we knew no one else could possibly understand the intensity of our battle. Instead of watching television, we spent time reading Scripture. We listened to the Bible on audiotape around the clock, and we asked the nurses to come in at night and turn the tapes over.

In other words, we turned the hospital room into a sanctuary for God to dwell in. We kept the atmosphere charged with praise.

> *Let the saints be joyful in glory; let them sing aloud on their beds. Let the high praises of God be in their mouth, and a two-edged sword in their hand.*　(Psalm 149:5–6)

We spent time praising the Lord and discovered the awesome power of praise. God inhabits the praises of His people. (See Psalm 22:3 KJV.) Praise brings God's presence on the scene. When Paul and Silas were in prison, they decided to sing praises. By changing the atmosphere, they changed their circumstances. (See Acts 16:22–34.) Praise causes chains to break and walls to fall! And, praise paralyzes the enemy. (See Psalm 8:2.)

Praise brings God's presence on the scene. Praise causes chains to break and walls to fall!

Our friends, the Koesters, came to the hospital with their guitar one day, and we sang songs together and played Nerf basketball. We loved it, and others in the hospital loved it, as well, because it dispelled the atmosphere of gloom and doom.

Praise music will lift your spirit. If you don't know what to sing, open your Bible to the book of Psalms. Find the words in a psalm and begin to make up a melody and sing to the Lord. Psalm 136, for example, is a psalm in which Israel praised God for His power, mercy, and victories.

Most people don't realize how powerful praise is in our arsenal of weapons. The enemy wants to load you down with his junk, but you can praise your way to freedom!

There were times when I didn't feel like praising the Lord, but I did it by faith.

> *The garment of praise for the spirit of heaviness.*
>
> (Isaiah 61:3)

There is the story of a woman who went to China years ago as a missionary. While there, she contracted smallpox. At the time, there was no cure for smallpox, and there was nothing that the doctors could do, so she was quarantined. As she sought the Lord, the Lord showed her two baskets. One basket was full; it represented her smallpox. The other basket was empty; it represented her praise. The Lord told her that when her praise basket got full, her healing would manifest.

The enemy has nothing to combat praise; he's powerless against it.

So, the missionary sang praises to God from her heart. She praised God for His greatness. She praised Him for His faithfulness. She praised Him for her healing. Finally, after several days, she was healed.

Praise is a powerful weapon. If you will begin to praise God in the morning, you will be amazed at what He will do. Even if you don't feel like praising Him, you can put on the garment of praise for the spirit of heaviness.

Praise changes us. It changes our attitudes. It changes our outlook. It takes our eyes off ourselves and puts them on God. Praise brings the presence of God on the scene.

Praise is like an atomic bomb or nuclear warhead—it causes the enemy to run in terror! The enemy has nothing to combat praise; he's powerless against it, because God inhabits our praises. Victorious Christians are those who have learned to praise.

The Joy of the Lord

God expects us to live our faith in front of the world, so we also set an atmosphere of joy in my hospital room. We were desperate for joy in the midst of the battle, because the Bible says, *"For the joy of the LORD is your strength"* (Nehemiah 8:10).

In the hospital, my father and I told jokes and recalled funny stories. In spite of all that I was going through—losing weight, having my hair fall out, and feeling sick—we always found things to be thankful for and to laugh about. You can always find something to laugh about, and laughter is good medicine. You can laugh your way to health.

In many hospitals, joke therapy has become common practice as nurses tell jokes to their patients. Research shows that laughter can heal heart disease and add years to your life. And the Bible says, *"A merry heart does good, like medicine, but a broken spirit dries the bones"* (Proverbs 17:22).

It's possible to have peace and joy in the midst of uncertainty and difficult circumstances. As I wrote about earlier, one time, I was so sick that I fell out of my bed while reaching for a cup. I landed with my head on the floor and my feet on the bed. Instead of crying, I began to say,

"Ha-ha-ha-ha-ha!" The nurse rushed into the room and said, "Are you all right?"

"Yes," I said. "I'm just laughing at these circumstances." The nurse must have thought I was crazy. I didn't *feel* like laughing, but I remembered what Rev. Jerry Savelle had said: "If Satan can't steal your joy, he can't take your goods!" I knew that if he couldn't steal my joy, he couldn't get my life.

There are times when you may feel more like crying than laughing, but you can yield to the joy of the Lord on the inside and say, "Ha-ha-ha!" *"The kingdom of God is...righteousness and peace and joy in the Holy Spirit"* (Romans 14:17).

One evening, a nurse brought a doctor into my room. She said, "This is the room I've been talking about." He stood in the middle of the room and looked around for a moment. Then, he said, "You're right! It *does* feel just like a church service in here!" After that, he turned and walked away.

I would say you're doing something right if you can turn a hospital room into a place of worship where the presence of God is tangible. We carry His presence everywhere we go. Greater is the presence of God in us than any sickness. The Bible says, *"Christ in you, the hope of glory"* (Colossians 1:27).

Now may the God of hope fill you with all joy and peace in believing, that you may abound in hope by the power of the Holy Spirit. (Romans 15:13)

Again, the enemy wants to load you down with his junk. But you can praise and laugh your way out of any situation because God has given you the victory.

Start by praising the Lord and laughing out loud for fifteen minutes a day.

Seven Promises from Psalm 91

Every day, confess Psalm 91 over yourself and your situation. In verses 14 through 16 of this psalm, there are seven things that God has promised He would do for those who love Him.

1. God Will Deliver Us

"Because he has set his love upon Me, therefore I will deliver him" (Psalm 91:14). Nothing is too hard for the Lord. No situation is so difficult that it will overtake us. With every situation, God has provided a way of escape.

He delivered Jonah from the belly of the whale. (See Jonah 1–2.) He delivered Shadrach, Meshach, and Abednego out of the fiery furnace. (See Daniel 3:8–30.) He delivered Daniel from the lions' den. (See Daniel 6.) He delivered an entire nation out of bondage. (See, for example, Exodus 12:29–41; 14–31.) Just as he delivered them, He can and will deliver you!

Many are the afflictions of the righteous, but the LORD delivers him out of them all. (Psalm 34:19)

Has God delivered you before? As He has done before, He will do again!

2. God Will Set Us On High

"I will set him on high, because he has known My name" (Psalm 91:14). There are many examples in the Bible where God took people from the lowest positions, raised them up, and set them in the highest positions—Joseph, David, and Saul's son, Mephibosheth, just to name a few.

In the book of Deuteronomy, God promised that if His people would obey Him, He would set them on high before all the nations of the earth. (See Deuteronomy 28:1 KJV.) We are to be the head and not the tail, always above and never beneath. (See verse 13.)

3. God Will Answer Us

"He shall call upon Me, and I will answer him" (Psalm 91:15.) People who have written books about God being silent or not answering prayer are either ignorant of God's Word or don't really know Him. God clearly promises that when we call upon Him, He will answer us, even though we may need to persevere at times.

Call to Me, and I will answer you, and show you great and mighty things, which you do not know.   (Jeremiah 33:3)

If you abide in Me, and My words abide in you, you shall ask what you desire, and it shall be done for you.   (John 15:7)

> **God promised that He would never leave us or forsake us.**

The enemy wants you to believe that God either doesn't hear your prayers or won't come through for you. God's purpose for creating man was for fellowship, to have a relationship with man. God hears every prayer and knows everything we go through. He is touched with the feeling of our infirmities. (See Hebrews 4:15 KJV.)

When we call upon Him, He will answer us and show us great and mighty things!

4. God Will Be with Us

"I will be with him in trouble" (Psalm 91:15.) One of Christ's names, *Immanuel*, means "God with us." (See Matthew 1:23.)

God is always with us, no matter where we are or what we're going through. He promised that He would never leave us or forsake us. (See, for example, Hebrews 13:5.) He lives inside us, and He is with us all the time. (See, for example, 1 Corinthians 3:16.)

5. God Will Honor Us

"*I will deliver him and honor him*" (Psalm 91:15). It's one thing to receive honor from men, but quite another to receive honor from the Lord. God promises to honor those who love Him. God also honors those who honor His Word. (See, for example, 1 Samuel 2:30; John 14:23.)

6. God Will Satisfy Us with Long Life

"*With long life I will satisfy him*" (Psalm 91:16). God's plan is for us to live long, fruitful lives. He wants us to have both quality of life and quantity of life. What is quantity of life without quality? And what is quality of life without quantity? He said He would satisfy us!

7. God Will Show Us His Salvation

"*And show him My salvation*" (Psalm 91:16). Again, in the New Testament, the Greek word translated "*saved*" is *sozo*. The word *sozo* refers to healing, wholeness, soundness, preservation, completeness. God said He would show us His salvation.

As you confess Psalm 91 over yourself and your situation, focus on these seven things God said He would do for those who love Him, and trust Him to fulfill them in your life.

CHAPTER FOURTEEN

Step Eight:
<u>Be Steadfast</u>

"Therefore, my beloved brethren, be steadfast, immovable,
always abounding in the work of the Lord, knowing that
your labor is not in vain in the Lord."
—1 Corinthians 15:58

There are times when we have to stand on God's promises no matter what we feel or see. If you expect to receive healing, you cannot be thinking that God is withholding healing from you because He has a greater purpose in mind. No, God purchased healing through Christ, and it now belongs to you. You must be steadfast to obtain God's promises. The word *steadfast* means "firmly fixed in place: immovable; firm in belief, determination, or adherence." Steadfastness is a requirement for winning and overcoming.

> *For we have become partakers of Christ if we hold the begin-*
> *ning of our confidence steadfast to the end.* (Hebrews 3:14)

> *For if we are faithful to the end, trusting God just as firmly*
> *as when we first believed, we will share in all that belongs to*
> *Christ.* (Hebrews 3:14 NLT)

We Are Qualified

When people have been in a lingering battle with illness, the enemy will often try to sabotage their faith. He'll tell them that they lack faith or that their faith is not working, simply because they haven't yet experienced the full manifestation of their healing. The enemy always works to make you feel insufficient, inadequate, and unqualified to receive from God.

The truth is that we *are qualified.*

> *Giving thanks to the Father who has qualified us to be partakers of the inheritance of the saints in the light.*
>
> (Colossians 1:12)

We are "more than conquerors" (Romans 8:37) through Jesus Christ.

The Bible says that God has given to every person *"a measure of faith"* (Romans 12:3). That measure is more than enough to cause us to overcome. We are *"more than conquerors"* (Romans 8:37) through Jesus Christ.

During my battle with Burkitt's lymphoma, there were many times when it would have been far easier to give up and quit. There were times when I didn't look healed and I sure didn't feel healed. I had fevers, infections, and complications. But whenever I listened to the Holy Spirit on the inside, He gave me the guidance and assurance I needed. One thing is sure: the Holy Spirit will not give up on you. He will encourage you to never give up or quit.

It's important that you continually put yourself in a position to read His Word and hear His voice.

> *And He said to them, Be careful what you are hearing. The **measure** [of thought and study] you give [to the truth you hear] will be the **measure** [of virtue and knowledge] that comes back to you—and more [besides] will be given to you who hear.* (Mark 4:24 AMP, emphasis added)

Again, be careful that you don't fall into a wrong mindset of "waiting" for your healing. Healing is *now*. Faith is *now*. *Today* is the day of salvation.

You must believe you receive your healing while continuing to hold on to your faith and remain confident and expectant that your healing is manifesting.

Healed "Speedily"

You must believe in God's power to heal. When the woman with the flow of blood wanted to be healed, she touched the hem of Jesus' clothing. (See, for example, Matthew 9:20–22.) Probably after hearing her account, others did the same thing.

> *And when the men of* [Gennesaret] *recognized Him, they sent out into all that surrounding region, brought to Him all who were sick, and begged Him that they might only touch the hem of His garment. And as many as touched it were made perfectly well.* (Matthew 14:35–36)

Something similar occurred later in Peter's ministry:

> *And believers were increasingly added to the Lord, multitudes of both men and women, so that they brought the sick out into the streets and laid them on beds and couches, that at least the shadow of Peter passing by might fall on some of them.* (Acts 5:14–15)

Years ago, when Aimee Semple McPherson preached, people traveled from miles around to hear her minister. People who were sick often said, "If I can just touch the brick of the building where Aimee Semple McPherson is ministering, I'll be healed." Countless numbers were healed under her ministry.

A minister once said, "You can have quick results if you build your faith for quick results." *"Faith comes by hearing, and hearing by the word of God"* (Romans 10:17). You can confess these Scripture verses and believe for your healing to manifest quickly:

> *Bow down Your ear to me, deliver me speedily! Be my Rock of refuge, a strong Fortress to save me!*   (Psalm 31:2 AMP)

> *Do not hide Your face from me in the day of my trouble; incline Your ear to me; in the day that I call, answer me speedily.*   (Psalm 102:2)

> *The captive exile and he who is bent down by chains shall speedily be released; and he shall not die and go down to the pit of destruction, nor shall his food fail.* (Isaiah 51:14 AMP)

> *Then your light shall break forth like the morning, Your healing shall spring forth speedily, and your righteousness shall go before you; the glory of the LORD shall be your rear guard.*   (Isaiah 58:8)

> *I tell you, He will defend and protect and avenge them speedily. However, when the Son of Man comes, will He find [persistence in] faith on the earth?*   (Luke 18:8 AMP)

Many people ask, "When will God heal me?" Well, He already has. What they really mean to say is, "When will my healing manifest?" Too often, people are walking by sight rather than walking by faith. (See 2 Corinthians 5:7.) If you are walking by faith, then you have already received healing on the inside. Keep God's promises percolating on the inside, and what's on the inside will manifest on the outside.

If you've prayed the prayer of faith, and you believe you've received your healing, then keep thanking God that you are healed. And, keep confessing, "The healing power of God is working mightily in my body. My body is recovering. I am getting stronger every day. I am getting better and better. My body is healed, in Jesus' name."

How do you go from "I believe that I receive" to "Here it is!"? Follow Abraham's example of faith in Romans 4:

- He believed God. (See verse 18.)
- He did not consider the age of his body or the deadness of Sarah's womb. (See verse 19.)
- He was strengthened in faith. (See verse 20.)
- He gave glory to God. (See verse 20.)
- He became fully convinced that what God promised He was also able to perform. (See verse 21.)

Every time you speak God's Word and continue to stand on God's promises, no matter what things look like, Satan can't stand it. He'll do anything he can to prevent God's Word from being sown in your heart. Be persistent and steadfast in speaking God's Word, no matter what.

Refuse to Compromise

The enemy will always try to get you to settle for less than God's best. Compromise is the language of the devil. Refuse to settle. I was at a church in Colorado where I prayed for a man with partial deafness in one ear. He was instantly healed the moment I prayed for him. The next night, he came back and said, "My healed ear is better than my good ear. I want my good ear to hear just as good as my healed ear!" So, I prayed for his good ear, and he could hear very well in both ears. The man refused to settle for less. Because he refused to settle for less, he was healed.

Our good friend Norwood Clemons is a survivor. He has faced a number of challenges and has battled and overcome several serious illnesses when having even just one of those sicknesses would have caused many people to have given up. In 1945, at nine years of age, he contracted polio and had to wear a brace from his hip to his toe. Several surgeries were performed to help stabilize his ankle but they were not effective. However, when he was eleven years old, a friend invited him to a healing service. After the service, he went home and went to bed. The next morning, he woke up, took the brace off, and laid his crutches down. He told his mother he was healed.

Norwood was indeed healed of polio. Later, he was healed after having had a heart attack. He has also been healed of a brain tumor, bladder cancer, and prostate cancer. During his thirty-five-year career, he took only three days off from work for sick leave. Norwood keeps going. He trusts God. He has learned to overcome. He has seen God perform many miraculous things in his life, and he is a walking testimony to the goodness of God. In every situation, He refuses to compromise or quit. He just keeps going in the power and provision of God. If God will do it for Norwood, He will do it for you.

Let us hold tightly without wavering to the hope we affirm, for God can be trusted to keep his promise.

(Hebrews 10:23 NLT)

So let us seize and hold fast and retain without wavering the hope we cherish and confess and our acknowledgement of it, for He who promised is reliable (sure) and faithful to His word. (Hebrews 10:23 AMP)

If you remain steadfast in your faith, God will be steadfast to perform His Word.

How to Remain Steadfast

The Israelites were not able to enter the Promised Land the first time because their hearts were not steadfast with God. How do you remain steadfast? What do you do when it seems as though your faith is not working?

Remember God's Faithfulness

God has a long track record, and He has never failed. No one who has put his trust in Him has been ashamed. (See Psalm 22:5.) Recount all the wonderful things God has done for you. God is faithful, and He is faithful to watch over His Word and perform it. (See Jeremiah 1:12 NASB.) Your healing will manifest if you don't quit.

> **God has a long track record, and He has never failed.**

You may want to document God's faithfulness to you in a notebook or journal. This will help you to focus on God and His goodness as you walk out your healing.

Keep Doing What You Know to Do

Keep attending to God's Word. Confess the healing Scriptures. Pray in the Spirit. Follow your heart. Take Communion. Whatever the Lord leads you to do, do it. According to Hebrews 11:6, God *rewards* those who diligently seek Him.

> *But without faith it is impossible to please and be satisfactory to Him. For whoever would come near to God must*

[*necessarily*] *believe that God exists and that He is the re-*
warder of those who earnestly and diligently seek Him
[*out*]. (Hebrews 11:6 AMP)

Keep Taking Ground

Have you ever heard the riddle "How do you eat an
elephant?" Answer: "One bite at a time." God often works as
we take one small step at a time. A few years ago, I prayed
for a woman in a wheelchair who had been paralyzed for ten
years. I asked her what other complications she had developed
as a result of her paralysis. She told me she had suffered with
bursitis in her shoulder, migraine headaches, and a
degenerative hip. I prayed for her migraines and God
instantly healed her. I pray for her bursitis and God instantly
healed her. I prayed for her hips and they began to move and
rotate—she felt a change in her body. Finally, when I went
to pray for her paralysis, she jumped out of the wheelchair
and began to run around the room! She had been instantly
healed.

If it feels like you're stuck in a rut, start by taking small
steps. One lady who was diagnosed with four types of
cancer began to use her faith against them one at a time.
She watched as God first healed her of breast cancer. Then,
He healed her of bone cancer. Next, He healed her of liver
cancer. And, finally, God healed her of brain cancer. Within
seven months, she was healed from the top of her head to the
soles of her feet. If your situation looks overwhelming, break
it down into a series of small steps.

You might start by believing for your headache to leave or
your appetite to return. You might believe God to help you
walk a few steps. It's okay to take small steps, but, whatever

you do, keep taking ground and moving forward.

Sometimes, we have to be honest with ourselves about the level of our faith. If you are trying to believe God for healing from cancer when you have never believed Him before for healing from a headache, start small and watch God move.

> *It's okay to take small steps, but keep taking ground and moving forward.*

Be Determined That You Will Win

Don't quit. Don't give up. When the pain seems unbearable and the doctor has said there's no hope, you have to find the strength to say, "I don't care how I feel or what others say. This, too, shall pass. I will win. I am healed by the stripes of Jesus!"

> *For we have become partakers of Christ if we hold the beginning of our confidence steadfast to the end.* (Hebrews 3:14)

Remain steadfast, and you will last. Persistence always pays off. If you just hold on, you will *"see the goodness of the LORD in the land of the living"* (Psalm 27:13).

The greatest enemy the Israelites faced was the temptation to walk by sight rather than by faith. The spies who investigated the Promised Land came back with a negative report. They said, "We saw the giants and the walled cities! We were like grasshoppers in their sight and in our sight." (See Numbers 13:28, 32–33 KJV.)

"We walk by faith, not by sight" (2 Corinthians 5:7.) You can't win a spiritual battle by keeping your eyes on the natural circumstances. You have to look to God and to His

Word until they appear like giants and the disease and its symptoms look like grasshoppers in comparison. Most breakthroughs come by keeping your foot on the accelerator. What you contend for is what you will have.

CHAPTER FIFTEEN

Step Nine:
<u>Have a Vision for Victory</u>

"Where there is no vision, the people perish."
—Proverbs 29:18 (KJV)

Real change begins when we start to see the promises of God on the inside before they manifest on the outside. In order to see yourself healed on the inside, your spiritual eyes must be enlightened after hearing God's Word. Faith not only *believes*, but it also *sees* the promises of God. You will rise only to the level where you can see yourself.

I once had a tennis coach who said, "If you don't think you'll win, you won't. You'll never surprise yourself by winning a match you're not sure you can win. You must be convinced that you'll win before you start the match."

For all the promises of God in Him are Yes, and in Him Amen, to the glory of God through us. (2 Corinthians 1:20)

All God's promises in Christ are sure. However, you have a choice. You can either see yourself in Christ or see yourself in crisis. You can see yourself healed, or you can see yourself sick. You can see yourself victorious, or you can see yourself defeated.

Whatever you see on the inside is what you'll experience on the outside.

As [a man] thinks in his heart, so is he. (Proverbs 23:7)

We must see ourselves the way God sees us.

Because as He is, so are we in this world.   (1 John 4:17)

God sees us in Christ. He sees us forgiven, as if we had never sinned. He sees us healed. He sees us one with Him. He sees us victorious.

For he raised us from the dead along with Christ and seated us with him in the heavenly realms because we are united with Christ Jesus.   (Ephesians 2:6 NLT)

Your healing is not based on the condition of your body. Your healing is based on your position in Christ. The Bible says that you are seated with Christ in *"the heavenly places, far above all principality and power"* (Ephesians 1:20–21).

Reach into the Unseen Realm

> *As you focus on the unseen realm and speak God's words into the atmosphere, you bring those things into manifestation in the seen realm.*

There is an unseen realm. The unseen realm, or spirit realm, is more substantial than this natural realm. Everything in the seen realm was created from the unseen realm. The seen realm is temporary—things are here today and gone tomorrow. The seen realm, which is physical, is subject to change.

It is only as you focus on the unseen realm and speak God's words into the atmosphere that you bring those things that are in the unseen realm into manifestation in the seen realm.

Creative miracles are found in the unseen realm. Angels are God's messengers who deliver miracles from heaven to earth. Heaven has "warehouses" stockpiled with human body parts—limbs, organs, whatever is needed. Those parts are ready to be released and brought to the earth by angels on assignment. The angels are waiting for a person to release words into the atmosphere and call into being what is needed.

God is moved not by need but by faith. If God were always moved by need, He would be moving everywhere and all the time. The force of faith is the hand that reaches into the unseen realm and brings things into the seen realm.

As you study the life of Jesus, you'll discover that He healed all types and degrees of sickness and disease. He went into Galilee and healed all who were sick. (See Matthew 4:23.) He went into Syria and healed all who were sick—He healed those *"who were afflicted with various diseases and torments, and those who were demon-possessed, epileptics, and paralytics"* (verse 24). He healed *"the lame, blind, mute, maimed, and many others"* (Matthew 15:30). He healed people who were born with deformities or whose limbs had been lost through diseases or accidents. He healed people who'd had body parts surgically removed.

God Can Perform Creative Miracles

I was on staff at a church where we prayed for a creative miracle for a young lady who'd had part of her cervix removed. She was distraught because she could never have children. However, God healed her. God performed a creative miracle by giving her a whole cervix. The doctors were shocked, and her story made it to the top physicians at MCV (Medical College of Virginia) Hospital in Richmond.

> *Greater is the power of God in us than the sickness on us or around us.*

The power of God brings change. Greater is the power of God in us than the sickness on us or around us. God's power is far greater than Satan's power. We need to learn what belongs to us and how to appropriate it. We need to understand how to tap into the power of God that is available to all.

No sickness or disease has power over you. Nothing has power over you unless you give it power. We have the power of God to remove sickness and restore life.

> *The Spirit of God, who raised Jesus from the dead, lives in you. And just as God raised Christ Jesus from the dead, he will give life to your mortal bodies by this same Spirit living within you.* (Romans 8:11 NLT)

God is still the Creator. If He can restore limbs and body parts that have been missing, He can do anything! All things are possible with Him. (See, for example, Mark 10:27.) If God could raise me up off my deathbed, He can raise you out of your circumstances.

Keep seeing yourself in Christ. Keep seeing yourself healed. Keep your eyes on the unseen realm and not on the seen realm.

Tackle Healing by Faith

I was teaching in a service once when a lady jumped out of her seat, ran to the front, and tried to tackle me. She missed, fell onto the floor, and laid there until the service was over. God was apparently ministering to her there.

Years later, I was ministering in a different church when a woman said, "You probably don't remember me, but several years ago, you were ministering in a church, and I came running to the front of the church and tried to tackle you."

"Oh yes, I do remember you."

"Well, I had an incurable disease. While you were ministering, I got so excited, I could see myself healed. I didn't want to have to wait, so I said to myself, *I'm going to take my healing.* That's when I jumped out of my chair and ran to the front." She'd been instantly healed by the power of God.

> *That is what the Scriptures mean when they say, "No eye has seen, no ear has heard, and no mind has imagined what God has prepared for those who love him." But it was to us that God revealed these things by his Spirit. For his Spirit searches out everything and shows us God's deep secrets.*
>
> (1 Corinthians 2:9–10 NLT)

How Faith Works

Faith perceives as real fact what is not revealed to the senses. That means you believe that you're healed even while the doctors, lab tests, and symptoms in your body are screaming a different story. I know it isn't the way our world works, but it *is* the way faith works. You believe it by faith and see it with your spiritual eyes long before you see your healing manifest in the natural.

You believe it by faith and see it with your spiritual eyes long before you see your healing manifest in the natural.

Much like athletes understand the power of visualization as they practice their movements to perform in competition, you must *see* yourself well.

Again, Proverbs 23:7 says, *"As [a man] thinks in his heart, so is he."* Another translation states, *"As a man thinks in his heart, so does he become"* (HCSB).

You will rise only to the level where you can *see* yourself.

You may recall that, at my bedside in the hospital at the NIH, I kept a framed picture of myself healthy and well. While others around me were sick and expecting to die, I would turn and look at my picture and say, "By His stripes, I am healed. I will not die but live and declare the works of the Lord."

Take Your Victory Laps

I would also often get out of bed at midnight and take laps around the hospital wing. As I passed the nurses' station, I would tell them, "I'm taking my victory laps! I don't plan on staying here much longer." Every time I took a step, I let myself imagine my leaving the hospital alive. I would say, "I'm one step closer to leaving this place!"

On the inside, I saw myself leave the hospital long before I was discharged. I saw myself playing tennis. I saw myself traveling the world and sharing my testimony. I saw myself serving God. And, as I saw it, I prophesied it and declared it.

Other people couldn't see what I saw. People won't be able to see what you see, either. They will think that you're foolish and in denial, just as they thought I was, but you can't let that stop you. Don't let their opinions move you out of faith. I didn't, and…well…*I'm alive!* No one is laughing at me now, and no one's opinion matters except yours and God's.

In some children's cancer wards, the patients are encouraged to draw pictures. They're told to draw the good cells in their bodies destroying the bad cells. That exercise is a powerful tool. Likewise, constant feeding on the Word of God will build an image within you of what belongs to you. You'll begin to see yourself the way God sees you.

After further meditation on God's Word, what you see on the inside will become more real than what is happening to you or around you. You'll get to the point where you will *know that you know* that you are healed. Nothing and no one will be able to convince you otherwise. You will become *fully assured* that what God has promised, He will perform.

> *With respect to the promise of God, he* [Abraham] *did not waver in unbelief but grew strong in faith, giving glory to God, and being fully assured that what God had promised, He was able also to perform.* (Romans 4:20–21 NASB)

The woman with the flow of blood whom Jesus healed was afflicted with a hemorrhage of some kind. The Bible said that she'd spent all she had on doctors but had gotten worse instead of better. (See Mark 5:25–26.) Long before that woman ever came into Jesus' presence, she saw herself touching the hem of His garment. She saw herself healed. *"For she kept saying, If I only touch His garments, I shall be restored to health"* (Mark 5:28 AMP).

This woman meditated on her healing. She saw her healing. She believed she would be healed, and she acted in accordance with her faith. And, according to the Bible, the woman was healed.

A New Way to See

I once ministered to a woman named Shelly who'd suffered through a ten-year battle with cancer. It had eaten away skin, bone, and tissue on one part of her face, and that part of her face was sunken. Over time, she learned the healing Scriptures and grew stronger in her faith. But when I asked if she could see herself healed on the inside, she said she couldn't.

So many years had passed that she couldn't relate to an old photo of herself, and she didn't have a recent one. I asked her to take a current photo. Then, we had someone take that photo and an old photo of her and transpose them to create a new photograph of her current face healed. When she saw the picture, she said, "Wow! Now, this is something I can relate to!" Over the next several months, as she meditated on the photo and on the promises of God, she was able to get a vision of herself healed. And, while she meditated on that picture, new bone, skin, and tissue grew back into her face. Her doctor couldn't believe the transformation.

> *But we all, with unveiled face, beholding as in a mirror the glory of the Lord, are being transformed into the same image from glory to glory, just as by the Spirit of the Lord.*
>
> (2 Corinthians 3:18)

Even after I was healed and released from the hospital, I was told that I would never run, never play tennis again, and never have children.

"It's too late," I responded. "I've already seen myself possessing those promises."

The enemy will always try to get you to settle for less than God's best. Refuse to settle! Get a vision of yourself coming out of that wheelchair. See yourself strong. See yourself healed. *"He who is in you is greater than he who is in the world"* (1 John 4:4).

Prophesy it, declare it over your life, and watch God bring it to pass!

> *But thanks be to God, who in Christ always leads us in triumph [as trophies of Christ's victory] and through us spreads and makes evident the fragrance of the knowledge of God everywhere.* (2 Corinthians 2:14 AMP)

Chapter Sixteen

Step Ten:

Make Plans

*"This is GOD's Word on the subject...'I have it all planned
out—plans to take care of you, not abandon you, plans to
give you the future you hope for.'"*
—Jeremiah 29:10–11 (MESSAGE)

When a couple finds out that they are going to have a
baby, what do they do? They begin to make plans
for when the baby will be born. They furnish and decorate
the nursery and buy diapers and baby clothes. Family and
friends hold a baby shower for them to make sure they have
everything they need—all before the baby arrives.

Faith works in the same way. At age nineteen, David
Yonggi Cho was a Korean Buddhist who'd been diagnosed
with a terminal case of tuberculosis. A young Christian
woman came each day to talk to him about the reality of
Jesus. He gave his life to the Lord Jesus and was healed of
tuberculosis. When God called him into the ministry, Cho
asked Him for a bicycle for transportation. As he meditated
on God's promises, God instructed him to see himself riding
the bike. Faith took root in his heart, and Cho described the
experience as being spiritually pregnant with a bicycle. By
faith, he was expecting! In time, the bicycle manifested in
the natural. Today, David Yonggi Cho is the pastor of the
world's largest church with more than 800,000 members.
Faith is full of expectancy. Faith begins to make plans for the
future. What great and glorious plans God has for your life!

As I lay in that hospital bed, I began to make plans for my future. I carried my healing in my heart much like a woman carries a baby. I told others what I would do as soon as I was released from the hospital. Faith always looks forward to the future.

> **I've witnessed the power of God heal people as soon as they began to do what God had called them to do.**

In the future, I imagined myself praying for the sick, so I began to pray for the sick in the hospital. My mother and I often went and prayed for others. We followed James 5:16, which says, *"Pray for one another, that you may be healed."*

I was pushing myself into my purpose. As you begin to push yourself into your purpose, the power of God will come on you and enable you to do what God has called you to do. I've witnessed the power of God heal people as soon as they took steps toward their purposes and began to do what God had called them to do. This is a powerful step and shouldn't be left out. Make plans! Set goals for your future!

Faith Looks Forward to the Future

I once ministered to a pastor who'd suffered a stroke and was paralyzed on one side of his body. He'd been bedridden for ten years, and his son had taken over the role of pastor of his church. After years of lingering illness, the pastor had become discouraged and depressed. He had refused to eat or get out of bed, and he had wasted away to a very frail man. He had stopped going to church. When I went to minister to him, he wouldn't respond to me. Instead, he glared off into space. When pressed, he told me that he wasn't interested in my praying for him.

"Pastor," I asked, "does that mean you've fulfilled your purpose? Have you finished your assignment?"

That got his attention. "No," he admitted.

"What would you do with your life if you were well and healed?" I asked, and he began to share some things.

"Have you prayed for the sick and seen miracles before?" I probed.

"Oh, yes!" he said.

"Tell me about all the miracles you have seen," I urged him. So, he sat up in the bed and began to tell me about miracles.

"What about your family?" I asked. "Don't you want to be able to enjoy your children and grandchildren?"

As the man realized that his purpose on earth was not finished and that there were still reasons for him to live, it engaged his will. When I prayed, the Lord healed his body. The next day, Sunday, just as I stood up to minister, he walked into the church—and the congregation went wild! We had a healing service that day, and he and I both laid hands on the sick. At the end of the service, people rejoiced and danced.

Ask yourself some questions. What would you do if you were healed? How would your life change? Get a sheet of paper and write down your future plans. Do you see yourself running again or riding a bike? How about going on a vacation? Do you like the beach or the mountains? Would you like to live long enough to enjoy time with your children and grandchildren? What about taking a mission trip? Sharing your testimony? Serving God in a greater way?

How about having a praise party to rejoice with others about your healing?

Dream God's Dream

You may not know your purpose, but as you follow God and start serving Him, His plan and purpose will unfold.

A year after I was healed, the Lord spoke to me and said, *Brian, you've had a dream in your heart, and for many years, you've been working to fulfill that dream. I want you to know I have a dream in My heart for you.*

I laid down my dream and took up God's dream. I found out that God's dream is more satisfying and rewarding than I ever imagined. I've never looked back, and I've never regretted that decision for a moment.

How about you? Are you ready? Will you surrender your will to God's will and make a commitment to Him that you will do whatever He wants you to do?

> *A man's heart plans his way, but the LORD directs his steps.*
> (Proverbs 16:9)

You may not know your purpose, but as you follow God and start serving Him, His plan and purpose will unfold. When God created us, He designed us with a plan in mind. We're not on this earth by accident or by mistake. God has plans to give us a future and a hope. (See Jeremiah 29:11 NIV.)

The Bible tells us,

> *For we are God's workmanship, created in Christ Jesus to do good works, which God prepared in advance for us to do.*
> (Ephesians 2:10 NIV)

> *For we are God's [own] handiwork (His workmanship), recreated in Christ Jesus, [born anew] that we may do those*

good works which God predestined (planned beforehand) for us [taking paths which He prepared ahead of time], that we should walk in them [living the good life which He prearranged and made ready for us to live].

(Ephesians 2:10 AMP)

God has a *"good life"* for us to live! He has prearranged for us to live the good life. The good life is a life free from sickness and disease.

One Scripture that helped to pull me through was this one: *"Being confident of this very thing, that He who has begun a good work in you will complete it until the day of Jesus Christ"* (Philippians 1:6). I knew from this verse that what God had started He would certainly finish. The Bible says that Jesus is *"the author and finisher of our faith"* (Hebrews 12:2).

Whom Shall I Send?

I heard the voice of the Lord, saying: "Whom shall I send, and who will go for Us?" Then I said, "Here am I! Send me." (Isaiah 6:8)

God needs our cooperation in order to accomplish His eternal plan. Several years ago, the Lord spoke to my wife and said, *I don't just have the plan or a plan for your life, but you are the plan.* The Lord reminded us of Noah, Moses, Esther, and Jesus. He showed us that they were not just part of God's plan; they *were* His plan.

"Whom shall I send, and who will go for Us?" God is still asking that question today. You and I are the plan of God. We are His plan to reach this generation. What God does in you and for you, He desires to do through you to reach many more people.

Some people want to be healed only to go back to their old lifestyles. I like what Peter's mother-in-law did when she was healed by Jesus. Immediately after she was healed, she arose and began serving. (See Matthew 8:14–15.)

> *We're living in one of the greatest times in human history. We'll see miracles, signs, and wonders that we've never seen before.*

Once she was healed, she began serving the Lord! The greatest thing you can do for God is to begin serving Him. Find out what He wants you to do and start doing it. If you're not sure where to start, the best place to begin is in your local church. Notice what the Scriptures tell us about Jesus: *"For even the Son of Man came not to be served but to serve others and to give his life…"* (Matthew 20:28 NLT).

God promises that if we seek first His kingdom and His righteousness, anything we need shall be added unto us. (See Matthew 6:33.) God *does* want you healed. Most important, God *wants you*. He wants your heart and your life, and He wants to use you for His glory.

The Time Is Now

We're living in one of the greatest times in human history. The signs are all around us. It's time for the greatest move of the Spirit of God that the world has ever known. God promises to visit us in the last days. This move of God will be a demonstration to the world of how awesome our God really is. We'll see miracles, signs, and wonders that we've never seen before. The glory of God will be demonstrated in greater measure than ever.

Step Ten: Make Plans

Arise, shine; for your light has come! And the glory of the LORD is risen upon you. For behold, the darkness shall cover the earth, and deep darkness the people; but the LORD will arise over you, and His glory will be seen upon you. The Gentiles shall come to your light, and kings to the brightness of your rising. Lift up your eyes all around, and see: they all gather together, they come to you; your sons shall come from afar, and your daughters shall be nursed at your side. Then you shall see and become radiant, and your heart shall swell with joy; because the abundance of the sea shall be turned to you, the wealth of the Gentiles shall come to you.

(Isaiah 60:1–5)

Get ready, get ready, get ready! Prepare yourself to see and to be a part of this great revival. Make plans, because God has a plan for you.

CHAPTER SEVENTEEN

Step Eleven:
Pray the Prayer of Faith

"And the prayer offered in faith will restore the one who is sick, and the Lord will raise him up, and if he has committed sins, they will be forgiven him."
—James 5:15 (NASB)

John Wesley said, "God does nothing but in answer to prayer."[3] It is not prayer alone but effective prayer that gets results. Many types of prayers are found in the New Testament. Ephesians 6:18 says, *"And pray in the Spirit on all occasions with **all kinds of prayers** and requests. With this in mind, be alert and always keep on praying for all the saints "* (NIV, emphasis added).

Thankfully, when I was a patient at the NIH, we had a church family and close friends who knew how to pray the prayer of faith. They knew how to pray in faith and to pray according to the Word of God. There are many kinds of prayer, and I believe each kind has its own set of spiritual laws. It's a lot like sports. Football, baseball, basketball, and soccer are all sports, but each has its own rules of engagement. The same is true with prayer, and sometimes we get into trouble when we mix and match the rules. For instance, in the garden of Gethsemane, Jesus prayed the prayer of consecration. This prayer is found in three of the

---

[3] E. M. Bounds, *Power through Prayer* (New Kensington, PA: Whitaker House, 1982), 117.

gospels. Let us look at how it reads in the *Amplified Bible* in the book of Matthew:

> *And going a little farther, He threw Himself upon the ground on His face and prayed saying, My Father, if it is possible, let this cup pass away from Me; nevertheless, not what I will [not what I desire], but as You will and desire.*
>
> (Matthew 26:39 AMP)

There is a lot of misunderstanding about this prayer. A tradition has developed of praying the prayer of consecration when praying for the sick. That's a misuse of this type of prayer. To clear up any misunderstanding, let me assure you that this was the only time in the New Testament when Jesus prayed this particular prayer, and He never prayed it when healing the sick. The other thing of note is that when Jesus and the apostles prayed for the sick, they used their authority; they didn't ask God to heal the sick. Here are some examples of this:

Praying with Authority

The Man with a Withered Hand

> *Jesus went into the synagogue again and noticed a man with a deformed hand. Since it was the Sabbath, Jesus' enemies watched him closely. If he healed the man's hand, they planned to accuse him of working on the Sabbath. Jesus said to the man with the deformed hand, "Come and stand in front of everyone." Then he turned to his critics and asked, "Does the law permit good deeds on the Sabbath, or is it a day for doing evil? Is this a day to save life or to destroy it?" But they wouldn't answer him. He looked around at them angrily and was deeply saddened by their hard hearts. Then*

*he said to the man, "Hold out your hand." So the man held
out his hand, and it was restored!* (Mark 3:1–5 NLT)

Notice that Jesus didn't pray to God to heal the man and
say, "If it be Thy will." In the Bible, you'll never find the
prayer of consecration used when praying for the sick. Let's
look at another example.

The Paralytic Man

*Jesus climbed into a boat and went back across the lake to his
own town. Some people brought to him a paralyzed man on
a mat. Seeing their faith, Jesus said to the paralyzed man,
"Be encouraged, my child! Your sins are forgiven." But some
of the teachers of religious law said to themselves, "That's
blasphemy! Does he think he's God?" Jesus knew what they
were thinking, so he asked them, "Why do you have such evil
thoughts in your hearts? Is it easier to say 'Your sins are forgiven,' or 'Stand up and walk'? So I will prove to you that
the Son of Man has the authority on earth to forgive sins."
Then Jesus turned to the paralyzed man and said, "Stand
up, pick up your mat, and go home!" And the man jumped up
and went home!* (Matthew 9:1–7 NLT)

Again, Jesus didn't ask God to heal the man or tack on to
His statement, "If it be Thy will."

The Blind Men

*After Jesus left the girl's home, two blind men followed
along behind him, shouting, "Son of David, have mercy on
us!" They went right into the house where he was staying,
and Jesus asked them, "Do you believe I can make you see?"
"Yes, Lord," they told him, "we do." Then he touched their*

eyes and said, "Because of your faith, it will happen."
(Matthew 9:27–29 NLT)

You may say, "Well, that was Jesus. Surely the apostles prayed in a different manner." Let's look at an example of how the apostles prayed in faith.

The Apostles Heal

One day Peter and John were going up to the temple at the time of prayer—at three in the afternoon. Now a man crippled from birth was being carried to the temple gate called Beautiful, where he was put every day to beg from those going into the temple courts. When he saw Peter and John about to enter, he asked them for money. Peter looked straight at him, as did John. Then Peter said, "Look at us!" So the man gave them his attention, expecting to get something from them. Then Peter said, "Silver or gold I do not have, but what I have I give you. In the name of Jesus Christ of Nazareth, walk." Taking him by the right hand, he helped him up, and instantly the man's feet and ankles became strong. He jumped to his feet and began to walk. Then he went with them into the temple courts, walking and jumping, and praising God.
(Acts 3:1–8 NIV, emphasis added)

The prayer of consecration is to be prayed anytime you're unsure of God's will. For instance, you can pray this prayer about what vocation to enter, whom to marry, or where to move. And, one of the most important times to pray the prayer of consecration is if you believe the Lord is calling you into ministry.

The reason it's dangerous to pray "If it be Thy will" when praying for the sick is that every kind of prayer requires faith. God's will on healing is made clear throughout the pages of the Bible. So, if you pray "If it be Thy will" when dealing with sickness, in effect, you're saying that you don't know what God's will is regarding healing. So, how could you be in faith? The Bible says that the only way to please God is through faith. (See Hebrews 11:6.) Don't mix and match the prayer of faith with the prayer of consecration.

Prayer Offered in Faith

The most common prayer for healing is the *"prayer of faith"* (James 5:15).

James told us that if a person is suffering, he should pray. He should call the elders (the pastor, deacons, and/or other spiritual leaders) to come and pray in faith:

> *Is anyone among you sick? Let him call for the elders of the church, and let them pray over him, anointing him with oil in the name of the Lord.* (verse 14)

Then, James gave us this assurance:

> *And the prayer of faith will save the sick, and the Lord will raise him up.* (verse 15)

James said the prayer of faith will heal the sick. He did not say that it *may* heal the sick but that it *will* heal the sick. He further stated,

> *And if he has committed sins, he will be forgiven.* (verse 15)

When we come to God, we receive His benefits—both forgiveness and healing. When we receive from Him, He doesn't want condemnation to enter into our thinking, because condemnation does not come from God.

> *For God did not send His Son into the world to condemn the world, but that the world through Him might be saved.*
> (John 3:17)

Satan is the accuser of the brethren. (See Revelation 12:10.) Yet, *"if we confess our sins, [God] is faithful and just to forgive us our sins and to cleanse us from all unrighteousness"* (1 John 1:9). The blood of Jesus washes us and makes us whole. We stand clean and righteous before God.

> *There is therefore now no condemnation to those who are in Christ Jesus, who do not walk according to the flesh, but according to the Spirit.* (Romans 8:1)

> [The Lord says], *I, even I, am He who blots out your transgressions for My own sake; and I will not remember your sins.* (Isaiah 43:25)

The enemy may try to bring those same thoughts of accusation again, and if he does, you just say, "I have already confessed that, and, in the name of Jesus, I am covered by the blood of Jesus. I am the righteousness of God in Christ Jesus." (See 2 Corinthians 5:21.)

Again, the enemy will try to make you feel unworthy, inadequate, and insufficient. Yet, Jesus Christ has not only purchased our redemption for us, but He has also made us qualified to receive the benefits of our redemption.

> *Giving thanks to the Father who has qualified us to be partakers of the inheritance of the saints in the light.* (Colossians 1:12)

You and I couldn't qualify on our own merits, and that's why God the Father sent His Son Jesus. Jesus is the only One who could qualify. And since He did, we do!

Just remember, Jesus healed sinners. In some individual cases, their sin had opened the door to sickness, but their sin could not prevent them from receiving healing. Why? Because grace is always greater than sin!

The Lord's mercies are new every morning. (See Lamentations 3:22–23.) *Healing is a mercy!* God wants us to receive everything He provided for us in Christ Jesus!

At the moment that you pray the prayer of faith, believe that you receive your healing. The word *receive* implies "take." You can *take* your healing because it belongs to you. And then go your way thanking God for it.

> *God wants us to receive everything He provided for us in Christ Jesus!*

How to Pray the Prayer of Faith

Here are some steps to help you pray the prayer of faith.

1. Before you pray, take time to meditate on the healing promises in order to establish a foundation for your faith.

2. Examine your heart: get your heart right with God and with others.

3. Meditate on the promises until you can "see" yourself healed.

4. Decide on a place/time to release your faith and believe you receive your healing, such as a healing service or prayer with your church elders.

5. At the moment you pray, believe that you receive or take your healing.

6. Expect a change in your body.

7. Thank the Lord for healing you and record the date/time you believed you received your healing.

CHAPTER EIGHTEEN

Step Twelve:
Faith, Medicine, and Doctors: Affirm Your Ultimate Source

"Asa became diseased in his feet, and his malady was severe; yet in his disease he did not seek the LORD, but the physicians. So Asa rested with his fathers; he died in the forty-first year of his reign."
—2 Chronicles 16:12–13

There are people who rely solely on doctors and medicine to heal their bodies. They spend countless hours researching diseases, specialists, and homeopathic remedies. Now, with so much information available on the Internet, it is very easy for people to become consumed with obtaining medical knowledge and to forget their ultimate source: God.

By contrast, there are others who feel that going to a doctor or taking medicine shows a lack of faith. They refuse to seek medical attention, avoid health insurance, and neglect the proper care of their bodies. They put both themselves and their families at great harm and risk.

How Do Faith, Doctors, and Medicine Work Together?

How do faith, doctors, and medicine work together? What does the Bible say on the subject?

God is not opposed to doctors or medicine. Jesus said, in effect, "Those who are sick need a physician." (See, for example, Mark 2:17.) If you're sick, then you need a doctor. Jesus Christ is the Great Physician. However, doctors and medicine can serve as a natural "helps ministry" (see 1 Corinthians 12:28) to Jesus' healing ministry.

The real issue involves trust. Who is your source? Who or what do you put your trust in?

If your trust is in man alone, the Scriptures say you are cursed:

> *Cursed is the man who trusts in man and makes flesh his strength, whose heart departs from the LORD.*
>
> (Jeremiah 17:5)

God never intended for us to put our trust in man. Thank God for medical advances that have helped so many people to live longer. But no man or medicine can heal you—they can only assist the body in the healing process.

King Asa died because *"he did not seek the LORD, but the physicians."* His trust was in the wrong place. His trust was not in the Lord. The danger is placing our faith and total trust in man or science rather than placing our total trust in the Lord.

> *Blessed is the man who trusts in the LORD, and whose hope is the LORD.* (Jeremiah 17:7)

The Question of Medicine

One question I get asked a lot is, "If I'm healed, should I throw away my medicine?" If you're healed, then go back to your doctor and have him confirm your healing. Let your physician make the decision that you no longer need medication.

Throwing away your medicine isn't a sign of whether you have great faith or not. Your faith is not in medicine; it's in God and rooted in His Word. Throwing away your medicine might be foolishness rather than faith. Let the doctor run tests and determine if your body is healed. Then, it will be a great testimony to him, as well as to others.

Jesus told the ten lepers to go and show themselves to the priests. In the Old Testament, a priest stood in the position of a doctor in pronouncing things as clean or unclean. No one showed himself to the priest unless he was healed. The ten lepers went on their way in faith to the priests, and as they did, they were cured. (See Luke 17:11–14.)

When I took medicine, the Lord directed my family and me to pray over every pill, injection, and IV, as well as each and every procedure.

When I took medicine, the Lord directed my family and me to pray over every pill, injection, and IV, as well as each and every procedure. We prayed, "This will do good and no harm, in Jesus' name." Our trust was in the Lord.

What about Surgery?

One question people often ask is, "If I have surgery or take chemo, how does God get the glory?"

It takes faith to believe God's Word, and it takes faith to have a doctor cut you open with a knife and to believe that all will go well. Nowhere in the Bible does it say that if you get medical attention, you turn off your faith. The Bible is not against taking the things of this world and using them in a constructive way.

> *He who does not use his endeavors to heal himself is brother*
> *to him who commits suicide.* (Proverbs 18:9 AMP)

If you undergo surgery, it doesn't mean you aren't in faith. You can believe that the surgery will go well, that the Lord will direct the surgeon's hands, that there will be no adverse complications, and that *"your healing shall spring forth speedily"* (Isaiah 58:8).

I've known people who were afraid of going to the doctor because they were afraid to hear what the doctor might say. Why not go to the doctor and find out what you are dealing with so that you can use your faith against it? *"God has not given us a spirit of fear, but of power and of love and of a sound mind"* (2 Timothy 1:7).

Be Prepared

However, if you go in for a test, procedure, or X-ray, go in spiritually prepared. Have your heart already fixed and established as to what you believe before you go.

> *He will not be afraid of evil tidings; his heart is steadfast,*
> *trusting in the LORD.* (Psalm 112:7)

Your faith doesn't rest in what the doctor says or what the test reveals, but in what God said.

Your faith doesn't rest in what the doctor says or what the test reveals, but in what God said. Keep your trust in God. Don't be moved by a negative report. Know that God's Word will not return void but will accomplish what it was sent forth to do. (See Isaiah 55:11.)

Believe God first. Follow the Lord's direction, and He will guide your steps. There have been times when the Lord has told me to go to the doctor and take medicine, and other times when He has told me not to go but to just stand on His Word or to take Communion and claim that I was healed. Every time I followed His instructions, I was healed. In the final analysis, if your trust is in the Lord, He will get the glory.

Sound Advice

- When choosing a doctor, choose one who is both skillful and positive with you, even if your prognosis appears grim in the natural. A "Christian" doctor may actually be more adversarial to your faith if he disagrees with your position on healing.

- When talking to the doctor, talk to him on his terms. Describe your symptoms. Be careful about using spiritual terminology that he may be unfamiliar with or that he may have no regard for.

- Remember that doctors are trained to look at medical facts, but God's Word is the truth.

- Beware of doctors who operate with fear, intimidation, or pressure. While God has not given you a spirit of fear and is not moved by pressure, you do have a choice regarding which doctor you select. It is both your prerogative and usually wise to get a second opinion.

- Lay out all of your options before the Lord, including those you may not particularly like, and be open to any direction the Lord shows you.

- Follow the leading and instructions of the Holy Spirit. Again, whatever He says, do it.

- Whatever course of medical treatment you decide on (surgery, medicine, and so forth), make your decision in faith and proceed in faith.

- If you do receive a negative report, go immediately into the presence of the Lord. Play inspirational music. Worship the Lord. Remember God's faithfulness. Remind yourself of what God has said to you and what He has promised in His Word.

- Before you go in for a test, X-ray, or appointment with the doctor, spend time praying in the Spirit. Know what you believe, based on God's Word, regardless of anything you hear, feel, or see.

- Believe God's report over man's report. *"Do not be afraid; only believe"* (Mark 5:36).

God Has Prepared Blessings for You

> *God wants you well and free of pain and disease much more than you want those things for yourself.*

God loves you to a depth that you can't even imagine. He loved you so much that Jesus was willing to die a cruel death on a cross to purchase both your eternal salvation and your healing. God isn't a hard taskmaster; He wants you well and free of pain and disease much more than you want those things for yourself.

Imagine yourself at a massive feast where tables are laden with delectable foods of every kind. Those foods are blessings that God has prepared for you. He's urging you to sit at the table He's made ready for you—right in the presence of your enemies. (See Psalm 23:5.) Feast at His table. *"Taste and see that the LORD is good"* (Psalm 34:8). Bask in His love and receive your healing.

Live long and enjoy the goodness of God.

Part III
Receiving Your Healing

Godly Instructions for Healing[4]

In order to understand these spiritual instructions, it helps if you have received Jesus as your Lord and Savior, a process we call being "born again" because it causes your spirit to be reborn in Christ. (See John 3:1–18.) In addition, it helps to pray and ask God to baptize you with His Holy Spirit, so that the Lord will be able to illuminate spiritual principles to you in a way that you can understand them. (See, for example, Mark 1:7–8; Acts 1:4–5; Acts 2:1–4; Acts 19:4–6.)

No matter how you feel led to proceed for your healing as you believe for God's miraculous intervention, whether through medicine, therapy, surgery, or a combination of things, as I did, use these principles. They're necessary to produce victory.

1. There is great power in the name of Jesus, so say it often. Say it in love; say it for help; say it for comfort; declare it for power; say it to stand against pain, doubt, and fear; and use its authority in prayer. (See, for example, John 14:12–14.)

2. The gap between man and God was bridged by the blood that Jesus shed on the cross for the forgiveness of our sins. It was that blood that allows believers into the presence of the Lord. There is tremendous power in both the name of Jesus and His blood. Invoking the blood of Jesus calls God onto the scene and causes the devil to flee. The blood of Jesus also provides

---

[4] These instructions for healing are based on a list given to me by Bob and Betty Anne Howell when I was in the hospital, which I have adapted and expanded.

protection, so pray the protective power of Jesus' blood over yourself, your family, your home, or your hospital room to clean out demonic forces.

3. When you receive the baptism of the Holy Spirit, you will receive a new prayer language. (See, for example, Mark 16:17.) The Bible says that praying in the Spirit will build you up, so do it often—even if you don't feel like it. (See, for example, Ephesians 6:18; Jude 1:20.) Always use your prayer language when battling panic or depression.

4. Pray a "foxhole" prayer. This prayer is a promise to the Lord that you'll follow His plan for your life and not your own. Commit to God that you will go where He wants you to go and do whatever He asks you to do, whether that means preaching the gospel or simply telling others about His goodness. Let Him know that your life is His.

5. Sometimes, we spend so much time asking God for help that we forget to be still and listen to what He's saying. Ask the Lord to give you a *rhema* word regarding your situation. This is a present word from God that He will speak in a still, small voice on the inside of you. A *rhema* word will always agree with the Bible. To receive this word, it helps to get still and quiet…and listen. When you receive His instructions, you can hang on to them and know with assurance the will of God.

6. Confidence in the Lord will bring you to a place of rest in the middle of the storm that swirls around you. Staying in that rest requires diligent work by being consistent, filled with hope and high expectations.

7. When family or friends come to visit you, instead of using the time to socialize, ask them to read to you. Keep things on hand that will build your faith. You can ask them to read the Bible, healing Scriptures, faith teachings, or anything else that is positive, encouraging, and uplifting.

8. Listen to the Bible, on CD or tape, to teachings about healing, and to praise music as much as possible. Even when you're busy doing other things, listen to the Word of God. You might get earphones so that you can go to sleep listening to the Bible on CD or tape. This will help it to get into your heart without distractions.

9. Anytime you're going to sleep, whether a natural or drug-induced sleep, commit your spirit, soul, and body into the hands of the Lord.

10. Spend your time giving thanks to God, and don't waste time talking to the devil. However, resist the devil (see James 4:7; 1 Peter 5:8–9) and command him to leave whenever the Lord prompts you to do so.

11. Healing doesn't fall from the sky. It starts on the inside of you and works its way to the outside. When you pray, don't repeatedly mention the problem or ask God why the illness is happening to you. Instead, be confident about what God has done for you and pray the results. Speak to the mountain of sickness and command that it be cast into the sea. (See, for example, Matthew 21:21–22.) In addition, something happens each time positive prayers go forth to God, so invite healing prayers by strong Christians.

12. There is a spiritual principle that you will receive what you give. (See Luke 6:38.) So, pray for other people. Lay hands on the sick, and you'll *both* recover.

13. Love Jesus more each day. Develop an intimate relationship with Him so that He is your friend and constant companion. Because of His sacrifice on the cross, you have a way out of your situation, so be grateful and thank Him often. Worst-case scenario, if you don't receive the manifestation of your prayers, you will go to be with Him. Whatever happens, Jesus should be your first love.

14. The Bible promises that the Word of God will not return void (see Isaiah 55:11) and that praise will drive away despair (see Isaiah 61:3). So, memorize Scriptures and sing anointed songs, because Jesus will lift your heart.

15. Listen to what the doctors and nurses have to say, being both respectful and obedient. But don't accept negative words into your heart and believe them. Never forget that you are under a higher authority—God's authority—and that nothing is impossible with Him.

16. Be wise enough not to push yourself too hard or too fast. If you are undergoing chemotherapy or other intense treatment or battling pain, pace yourself. Use your times of energy and alertness to attend to God's Word—reading it, speaking it, and exercising your faith through action. It is fine to rest your body and regroup. However, do not allow yourself to become passive and stop fighting. When you are regrouping, either sleep or rest. When you are resting, you can play CDs of faith-filled worship and praise music or Scripture.

17. Make plans, with the Lord's direction, for what you're going to do when your battle with sickness is over and

you're completely well. Imagine yourself carrying out those plans. Let faith and hope paint a picture of a wonderful future ahead.

18. Don't let the past haunt you. The enemy would like for you to get caught in the trap of thinking about what might have been if you hadn't gotten sick. Don't get caught in that snare. Rather, let the old things pass away and allow yourself to get excited about the new things God has in store for you.

19. The Bible tells us to put on the whole armor of God. Study Ephesians 6:10–18 and, by faith, daily dress yourself with the belt of truth and the breastplate of righteousness. Shoe your feet with the preparation of the gospel of peace. Put on the helmet of salvation and take up the shield of faith and the sword of the Spirit, which is the Word of God.

20. What you say is what you get, so guard every word that comes out of your mouth. There's great power in words, so "predict" your victory, calling it into existence as you quote the Word of God.

21. It's crucial that you get right with others and walk in love. Ask the Lord to reveal any unforgiveness, bitterness, or resentment that may be hidden in your heart. These are more deadly than any disease, so confess them as sin and repent to God and to others.

22. Plead your case with God. Remind Him that your family needs you spiritually, emotionally, physically, and financially. Tell Him that you want to see your children grow up and mature in the Lord and that you are a benefit to the body of Christ.

23. Go to anointed meetings whenever you get the chance. Signs and wonders follow the anointed teaching of

the Word of God, and, often, the gifts of the Spirit of God are present to heal.

24. Call prayer groups and ask them to pray with you. Start with prayer groups in your church or community, but don't stop there. Call national prayer lines, as well, such as *The 700 Club*, Oral Roberts Prayer Tower, and others. Do not call people and ask for prayer if they don't believe healing is promised in the Bible.

25. Take Communion by yourself or with others. The Bible says, *"By* [His] *stripes you were healed"* (1 Peter 2:24). That means that Jesus' body was broken to obtain your healing. Taking Communion is an act of covenant and reminds God of Jesus' shed blood and broken body, which paid the price for your healing. Always repent of any known sin before taking Communion, and also ask the Lord to reveal any hidden sin in your life so that you may confess and repent of it.

26. Tithing is another covenant act, so make sure you tithe 10 percent of your income to the Lord. The Bible says that if we tithe, God will rebuke the devourer for us. (See Malachi 3:11.) Sickness doesn't come from God; it comes from the devourer, Satan. Tithing activates God on our behalf.

27. Many people are stunned to learn that two of the major sins God hates are murmuring and complaining. Those sins are as deadly today as they were when Moses brought Israel out of Egypt. If you're not sure how God responds to murmuring and complaining, read the biblical account in Exodus of Israel's trip through the wilderness. Don't be negative or blame

God for what has happened. Murmuring and self-pity will destroy your faith and stop the answer to your prayers. Instead, be steadfast and thankful, trusting your Father more than you trust the symptoms, the diagnosis, or the prognosis.

Healing Confessions: Scriptures on Healing and Wholeness

*I am the L*ORD *who heals you.* (Exodus 15:26)

Surely He has borne our griefs (sicknesses, weaknesses, and distresses) and carried our sorrows and pains [of punishment]. (Isaiah 53:4 AMP)

He was wounded for our transgressions, He was bruised for our iniquities; the chastisement for our peace was upon Him, and by His stripes we are healed. (Isaiah 53:5)

When evening had come, they brought to Him [Jesus] many who were demon-possessed. And He cast out the spirits with a word, and healed all who were sick, that it might be fulfilled which was spoken by Isaiah the prophet, saying: "He Himself took our infirmities and bore our sicknesses." (Matthew 8:16–17)

[Jesus] Himself bore our sins in His own body on the tree, that we, having died to sins, might live for righteousness; by whose stripes you were healed. (1 Peter 2:24)

Christ has redeemed us from the curse of the law, having become a curse for us (for it is written, "Cursed is everyone who hangs on a tree"), that the blessing of Abraham might come upon the Gentiles in Christ Jesus, that we might receive the promise of the Spirit through faith. (Galatians 3:13–14)

10 Hours to Live

Bless the LORD, O my soul, and forget not all His benefits: who forgives all your iniquities, who heals all your diseases.
(Psalm 103:2–3)

"For I will restore health to you and heal you of your wounds," says the LORD. (Jeremiah 30:17)

With men it is impossible, but not with God; for with God all things are possible. (Mark 10:27)

My son, give attention to my words; incline your ear to my sayings. Do not let them depart from your eyes; keep them in the midst of your heart; for they are life to those who find them, and health to all their flesh. (Proverbs 4:20–22)

So shall My word be that goes forth from My mouth; it shall not return to Me void, but it shall accomplish what I please, and it shall prosper in the thing for which I sent it.
(Isaiah 55:11)

I am watching over My word to perform it.
(Jeremiah 1:12 NASB)

For all the promises of God in Him are Yes, and in Him Amen, to the glory of God through us. (2 Corinthians 1:20)

He sent His word and healed them, and delivered them from their destructions. (Psalm 107:20)

Then your light shall break forth like the morning, Your healing shall spring forth speedily, and your righteousness shall go before you; the glory of the LORD shall be your rear guard. (Isaiah 58:8)

Healing Confessions: Scriptures on Healing and Wholeness

I call heaven and earth as witnesses today against you, that I have set before you life and death, blessing and cursing; therefore choose life, that both you and your descendants may live; that you may love the LORD your God, that you may obey His voice, and that you may cling to Him, for He is your life and the length of your days; and that you may dwell in the land which the LORD swore to your fathers, to Abraham, Isaac, and Jacob, to give them. (Deuteronomy 30:19–20)

This Book of the Law shall not depart from your mouth, but you shall meditate in it day and night, that you may observe to do according to all that is written in it. For then you will make your way prosperous, and then you will have good success. Have I not commanded you? Be strong and of good courage; do not be afraid, nor be dismayed, for the LORD your God is with you wherever you go. (Joshua 1:8–9)

I shall not die, but live, and declare the works of the LORD. (Psalm 118:17)

So you shall serve the LORD your God, and He will bless your bread and your water. And I will take sickness away from the midst of you. No one shall suffer miscarriage or be barren in your land; I will fulfill the number of your days. (Exodus 23:25–26)

For the eyes of the LORD run to and fro throughout the whole earth, to show Himself strong on behalf of those whose heart is loyal to Him. (2 Chronicles 16:9)

Those who seek the LORD shall not lack any good thing. (Psalm 34:10)

If any of you lacks wisdom, let him ask of God, who gives to all liberally and without reproach, and it will be given to him. (James 1:5)

No evil shall befall you, nor shall any plague come near your dwelling....."Because he has set his love upon Me, therefore I will deliver him; I will set him on high, because he has known My name. He shall call upon Me, and I will answer him; I will be with him in trouble; I will deliver him and honor him. With long life I will satisfy him, and show him My salvation." (Psalm 91:10, 14–16)

Every good gift and every perfect gift is from above, and comes down from the Father of lights, with whom there is no variation or shadow of turning. (James 1:17)

If you then, being evil, know how to give good gifts to your children, how much more will your Father who is in heaven give good things to those who ask Him! (Matthew 7:11)

He who did not spare His own Son, but delivered Him up for us all, how shall He not with Him also freely give us all things? (Romans 8:32)

God anointed Jesus of Nazareth with the Holy Spirit and with power, who went about doing good and healing all who were oppressed by the devil, for God was with Him. (Acts 10:38)

The thief does not come except to steal, and to kill, and to destroy. I have come that they may have life, and that they may have it more abundantly. (John 10:10)

Healing Confessions: Scriptures on Healing and Wholeness

And Jesus went about all Galilee, teaching in their synagogues, preaching the gospel of the kingdom, and healing all kinds of sickness and all kinds of disease among the people. Then His fame went throughout all Syria; and they brought to Him all sick people who were afflicted with various diseases and torments, and those who were demon-possessed, epileptics, and paralytics; and He healed them.
(Matthew 4:23–24)

And behold, a leper came and worshiped Him [Jesus], saying, "Lord, if You are willing, You can make me clean." Then Jesus put out His hand and touched him, saying, "I am willing; be cleansed." Immediately his leprosy was cleansed.
(Matthew 8:2–3)

Jesus went about all the cities and villages, teaching in their synagogues, preaching the gospel of the kingdom, and healing every sickness and every disease among the people.
(Matthew 9:35)

Then great multitudes came to Him, having with them the lame, blind, mute, maimed, and many others; and they laid them down at Jesus' feet, and He healed them. So the multitude marveled when they saw the mute speaking, the maimed made whole, the lame walking, and the blind seeing; and they glorified the God of Israel. (Matthew 15:30–31)

Jesus Christ is the same yesterday, today, and forever.
(Hebrews 13:8)

Most assuredly, I say to you, he who believes in Me, the works that I do he will do also; and greater works than these he will do, because I go to My Father. (John 14:12)

And He said to them, "Go into all the world and preach the gospel to every creature. He who believes and is baptized will be saved; but he who does not believe will be condemned. And these signs will follow those who believe: In My name they will cast out demons; they will speak with new tongues; they will take up serpents; and if they drink anything deadly, it will by no means hurt them; they will lay hands on the sick, and they will recover." (Mark 16:15–18)

A multitude gathered from the surrounding cities to Jerusalem, bringing sick people and those who were tormented by unclean spirits, and they were all healed.

(Acts 5:16)

I tell you the truth, whatever you forbid on earth will be forbidden in heaven, and whatever you permit on earth will be permitted in heaven. (Matthew 18:18 NLT)

For assuredly, I say to you, whoever says to this mountain, "Be removed and be cast into the sea," and does not doubt in his heart, but believes that those things he says will be done, he will have whatever he says. (Mark 11:23)

Therefore I say to you, whatever things you ask when you pray, believe that you receive them, and you will have them. And whenever you stand praying, if you have anything against anyone, forgive him, that your Father in heaven may also forgive you your trespasses. (Mark 11:24–25)

Again I say to you that if two of you agree on earth concerning anything that they ask, it will be done for them by My Father in heaven. (Matthew 18:19)

Healing Confessions: Scriptures on Healing and Wholeness

If you abide in Me, and My words abide in you, you shall ask what you desire, and it shall be done for you. (John 15:7)

Now this is the confidence that we have in Him, that if we ask anything according to His will, He hears us.
(1 John 5:14)

Is anyone among you sick? Let him call for the elders of the church, and let them pray over him, anointing him with oil in the name of the Lord. And the prayer of faith will save the sick, and the Lord will raise him up. And if he has committed sins, he will be forgiven. (James 5:14–15)

Without faith it is impossible to please Him, for he who comes to God must believe that He is, and that He is a rewarder of those who diligently seek Him. (Hebrews 11:6)

For we walk by faith, not by sight. (2 Corinthians 5:7)

Since we have the same spirit of faith, according to what is written, "I believed and therefore I spoke" we also believe and therefore speak. (2 Corinthians 4:13)

With respect to the promise of God, he [Abraham] did not waver in unbelief but grew strong in faith, giving glory to God, and being fully assured that what God had promised, He was able also to perform. (Romans 4:20–21 NASB)

Fear not, for I am with you; be not dismayed, for I am your God. I will strengthen you, Yes, I will help you, I will uphold you with My righteous right hand. (Isaiah 41:10)

Do not be afraid; only believe.   (Mark 5:36)

Beloved, I pray that you may prosper in all things and be in health, just as your soul prospers.   (3 John 2)

Therefore take up the whole armor of God, that you may be able to withstand in the evil day, and having done all, to stand. Stand therefore, having girded your waist with truth, having put on the breastplate of righteousness, and having shod your feet with the preparation of the gospel of peace; above all, taking the shield of faith with which you will be able to quench all the fiery darts of the wicked one. And take the helmet of salvation, and the sword of the Spirit, which is the word of God; praying always with all prayer and supplication in the Spirit, being watchful to this end with all perseverance and supplication for all the saints.

(Ephesians 6:13–18)

You are awesome, O God, in your sanctuary; the God of Israel gives power and strength to his people. Praise be to God!   (Psalm 68:35 NIV)

Casting down imaginations and every high thing that exalts itself against the knowledge of God, bringing every thought into captivity to the obedience of Christ.

(2 Corinthians 10:5)

For God has not given us a spirit of fear, but of power and of love and of a sound mind.   (2 Timothy 1:7)

"No weapon formed against you shall prosper, and every tongue which rises against you in judgment you shall

condemn. This is the heritage of the servants of the LORD, and their righteousness is from Me," says the LORD.
(Isaiah 54:17)

A merry heart does good, like medicine, but a broken spirit dries the bones. (Proverbs 17:22)

For the joy of the LORD is your strength. (Nehemiah 8:10)

Peace I leave with you, My peace I give to you; not as the world gives do I give to you. Let not your heart be troubled, neither let it be afraid. (John 14:27)

May the God of hope fill you with all joy and peace in believing, that you may abound in hope by the power of the Holy Spirit. (Romans 15:13)

You will keep in perfect peace all who trust in you, all whose thoughts are fixed on you! (Isaiah 26:3 NLT)

The Spirit of God, who raised Jesus from the dead, lives in you. And just as God raised Christ Jesus from the dead, he will give life to your mortal bodies by this same Spirit living within you. (Romans 8:11 NLT)

Whatever they plot against the LORD he will bring to an end; trouble will not come a second time. (Nahum 1:9 NIV)

We have become partakers of Christ if we hold the beginning of our confidence steadfast to the end. (Hebrews 3:14)

Therefore do not cast away your confidence, which has great reward. (Hebrews 10:35)

10 Hours to Live

I can do all things through Christ who strengthens me.
(Philippians 4:13)

Surely there is a hereafter, And your hope will not be cut off.
(Proverbs 23:18)

Thanks be to God, who gives us the victory through our Lord Jesus Christ. (1 Corinthians 15:57)

About the Author

Brian Wills and his wife, Beth, are itinerant missionaries whose vision is to bring hope and healing to this generation. Through their ministry, Healing For The Nations, they have corporately traveled to over thirty-five nations of the world.

As ordained ministers, Brian and Beth travel and speak in Christian churches of all denominations and sizes. They primarily teach on faith, healing, revival, and knowing who you are in Christ.

Brian is a conference speaker and conducts healing services and workshops. His passion is to train others on "how to do the works of Jesus." Through practical teaching and demonstration, he believes every Christian can live a supernatural life. By the miracles he has witnessed, he has seen people's lives forever transformed by the power of God.

Brian graduated with honors from Drury University with a B.A. in business administration. While at Drury, he became a National Association of Intercollegiate Athletics (NAIA) nationally ranked tennis player and, at the time, the player with the most wins in school history.

In his early twenties, he was miraculously healed of Burkitt's lymphoma, a rare, usually fatal cancer of the lymph system. In 1987, the National Cancer Institute recognized his remarkable story and used his photo and story for promotional purposes. His testimony has been featured on Kenneth Copeland's *Voice of Victory* and Pat Robertson's *The 700 Club* and in several well-known newspaper and tennis publications.

Brian spent over twenty years in the tennis industry as a player, teacher, and coach. As a player, he competed on the European Pro Satellite and Challenger circuits. As an instructor, he has trained hundreds of ranked junior players and instructors and conducted clinics with well-known players and celebrities. Within the United States Tennis Association, he has served as an executive director, national clinician, and national coach. In 1990, Yamaha Sports voted him as one of the Top 5 teaching pros in the Mid-Atlantic region.

Brian and Beth are 1992 graduates of Rhema Bible Training Center in Broken Arrow, Oklahoma. While attending Rhema, Brian served as a volunteer for the Prayer and Healing Center and at the Healing School. Beth served as a volunteer in the publications department for Kenneth Hagin Ministries.

Today, Brian is a guest instructor at Rhema Bible Training Centers overseas, as well as other Bible schools around the world. Brian and Beth reside near Richmond, Virginia, and have four children: Madeline, Emily, Jessica, and Preston.

Brian and Beth Wills are available to speak anywhere in the U.S. and overseas. For more information, please contact:

Brian and Beth Wills
Healing For The Nations
P.O. Box 6034
Ashland, VA 23005

E-mail: healingnations@comcast.net
Web sites: www.healing4nations.com;
www.10hourstolive.com
Phone: (804) 798-4498

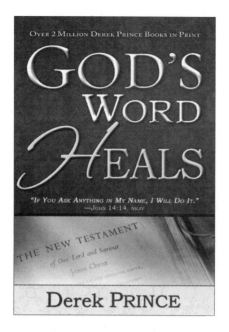

God's Word Heals
Derek Prince

From best-selling author and Bible teacher Derek Prince comes his most detailed teaching on God's miraculous gift of healing. Writing from decades of ministry experience as well as his own miraculous healing, Prince explains how God heals. He shows the Bible's easy-to-follow guidelines so you can apply God's instructions for your complete healing.

ISBN: 978-1-60374-210-8 • Trade • 256 pages

WHITAKER
HOUSE

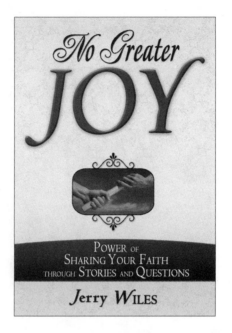

No Greater Joy
Jerry Wiles

Through personal illustrations from years of effective witnessing and solid biblical teaching, Jerry Wiles shows how you can see powerful results in the lives of others and…

• Recognize opportunities for sharing the gospel
• Ask questions to start spiritual conversations
• Know what not to say or ask
• Eliminate fears and other hurdles
• Demonstrate God's power and love

ISBN: 978-1-60374-242-9 • Trade • 240 pages

WHITAKER
HOUSE